Zen in Ten

Ten Easy
Lessons Series

Zen in Ten

C. Alexander Simpkins, Ph.D.
&
Annellen M. Simpkins, Ph.D.

Tuttle Publishing
Boston · Rutland, VT · Tokyo

First published in 2003 by Tuttle Publishing, an imprint of Periplus Editions (HK) Ltd., with editorial offices at 153 Milk Street, Boston, Massachusetts 02109.

Grateful acknowledgement is made for permission to reprint previously published material:

Japanese Death Poems compiled by Yoel Hoffman. Copyright © 1986 by Charles E. Tuttle Co., Inc. By permission of Tuttle Publishing.

Zen Art for Meditation by Stewart W. Holmes and Chimyou Horioka. Copyright © 1973 by Charles E. Tuttle Co., Inc. By permission of Tuttle Publishing.

The Zen Poetry of Dōgen by Steven Heine. Copyright © 1997 by Steven Heine. By permission of the author.

Library of Congress Cataloging-in-Publication Data

Simpkins, C. Alexander.
    Zen in ten / by C. Alexander Simpkins & Annellen M. Simpkins
       p. cm. — (Ten easy lessons series; 2)
    Includes bibliographic references.
    ISBN: 0–8048–3450–4 (pbk.)
       1. Religious Life—Zen Buddhism. 2. Zen Buddhism—Doctrines. I. Simpkins, Annellen
M. II. Title. III. Series.

BQ9286 . S56 2003
294 . 3' 927—dc21   2002075059

Distributed by:

North America
Tuttle Publishing
Distribution Center
Airport Industrial Park
364 Innovation Drive
North Clarendon, VT 05759-9436
Tel: (802) 773-8930
Fax: (802) 773-6993
Email: info@tuttlepublishing.com
Web site: www.tuttlepublishing.com

Indonesia
PT Java Books Indonesia
Jl. Kelapa Gading Kirana
Blok A14 No. 17
Jakarta 14240 Indonesia
Email: cs@javabooks.co.id

Asia Pacific
Berkeley Books Pte. Ltd.
130 Joo Seng Road
#06-01/03 Olivine Building
Singapore 368357
Tel: (65) 6280-3320
Fax: (65) 6280-6290
Email: inquiries@periplus.com.sg

Japan
Tuttle Publishing
Yaekari Building, 3rd Floor
5-4-12 Ōsaki, Shinagawa-ku, Tokyo
Japan 141-0032
Tel: (03) 5437-0171
Fax: (03) 5437-0755
Email: tuttle-sales@gol.com

First edition
08 07 06 05 04   9 8 7 6 5 4 3 2

Design by Dutton & Sherman Design
Printed in Canada

Contents

Preface

Count to Ten
And you'll be Zen!
                —C. Alexander Simpkins

Zen is a potent approach to mental development. Modern living
emphasizes achieving goals in the outer world, but sometimes it neg-
lects the inner world. Zen begins from the inner world, teaching a
sophisticated method for developing and working with the mind. As
awareness becomes more acute and disciplined, another way of performing actions emerges. Hobbies, relationships, and even work can
be mastered, not just gotten through. Each activity takes on added
meaning and becomes more fulfilling. By entering into the Zen Way,
you enrich the quality of your life, making every minute count.

About This Book

This book presents fundamental teachings of Zen in ten easy lessons.
Each lesson gives methods, principles, and understandings of Zen.

Beginning with meditation, you take your first step on the Zen path to inner development. With the lessons that follow, you come to understand the key issues and themes in Zen to guide you in mental skills. Later lessons introduce you to the traditional ways to expand awareness through the Zen arts. The final two lessons help you transform yourself and integrate Zen into your life. As these ten lessons teach you how to utilize the great potential of your own mind, infinite possibilities for better living emerge.

How to Use This Book

Zen is an experiential method, so each lesson gives ways for you to participate in Zen directly. Read a section and then try the exercises. Many of them incorporate meditation, since meditating is the core of Zen. We include varied approaches to developing meditation skills. Allow your thinking to be flexible and open. Most important, discover methods that help you enter and stay on your path.

We encourage you to use this book as a guide, a lantern to light the Way. Ultimately, Zen comes from within. Be patient and enjoy the journey!

Introduction

Historical Background
of Zen

Like dandelion seeds blown far away
On the gusty winds of chance
We little know where
Or what will become
In history's ground of circumstance
        —C. Alexander Simpkins

Buddhist Beginnings

The history of Zen is traced back to the enlightenment of one man, Siddhartha Gautama (563–483 B.C.). Siddhartha was an Indian prince raised with every luxury. But his sensitive nature felt compassion for those in his kingdom who suffered from poverty, illness, and death. Even though he seemed to have everything anyone could want, he felt powerless to prevent other people's suffering. So he gave up everything to pursue a spiritual life that might help him solve the problem of suffering.

Siddhartha spent his next years practicing ascetic self-denial while meditating in the forest. But this path did not lead him to find an end to suffering. Instead, he was dying of starvation. Recognizing that he would never find the answers he sought if he let himself die, he took some nourishment. Refreshed, he sat down under a bodhi tree (a kind of fig tree that grows in India), and vowed not to stop meditating until he solved the problem of suffering. He sat all night, deep in meditation. As the sun rose over the horizon, the explanation to life's miseries became crystal clear. With his enlightenment, Siddhartha became the Buddha, which means the awakened one, and Buddhism was born.

Gathering followers throughout India, Buddha spread his message of a middle way, a life of moderation between abstinence and indulgence. He taught how to tame the mind, for therein lay the only true path to happiness. Using meditation, people could learn to conquer the self.

One day, Buddha taught a large group of disciples at Vulture Peak in India. Everyone sat quietly and listened intently, trying to understand the deeper meaning of his speech. But Buddha did not tell them what to think. Instead, he ended his lesson by quietly holding up a flower. He looked out over the crowd and saw that only one monk, Mahakasyapa, smiled. This silent exchange between teacher and student was the first direct transmission of enlightenment. Direct transmission between Buddha and Mahakasyapa expressed the essence of Zen. The spirit of Zen began on that day.

Buddhism spread to many countries. Between the first and the third centuries, China received Buddhism. The Chinese had been steeped in Taoism and Confucianism for many centuries. Taoist and Confucian principles merged with Buddhism, setting the stage for Zen.

Bodhidharma

Traditionally, Bodhidharma (440–528) is credited as the founder of Zen. He lived in India and studied Buddhism under his teacher, Pranatara.

Bodhidharma Meditating Facing a Cliff. Late Song Dynasty (960–1279)
China. Hanging scroll, ink on silk. John L. Severance Fund,
The Cleveland Museum of Art.

His teacher's final wish was for Bodhidharma to take the message of meditation to China. Bodhidharma made the difficult journey to China and was disappointed in how Buddhism was practiced there. What's more, no one seemed interested in his pure form of meditation.

After unsuccessfully attempting to communicate with the emperor, Bodhidharma retired in discouragement to a cave. He sat facing a wall in meditation for nine years, until a student, Hui-k'o (487–593), convinced him to teach his committed methods to others. Bodhidharma taught the monks at the Shaolin temple not only to keep their minds clearly focused in meditation, but also to vitalize their practice through martial arts. Bodhidharma is also credited with founding martial arts, for he devised these movements to protect himself nonviolently on the long trip from India to China.

Bodhidharma taught that the awake, aware mind is already there. All people need to do is attune to it through devotion to meditation. Nothing else is needed.

> If someone is determined to reach enlightenment, what is the most essential method he can practice? The most essential method, which includes all other methods, is beholding the mind. But how can one method include all others? The mind is the root from which all things grow. If you can understand the mind, everything else is included. (Bodhidharma's *Breakthrough Sermon* in Pine 1989, 77)

Bodhidharma's teachings were transmitted directly, teacher to student, through five generations.

The Sixth Patriarch

Although Bodhidharma founded the Zen movement, Hui-neng (638–713), the Sixth Patriarch, led Zen in a new direction that is still followed today.

Hui-neng was an illiterate, uneducated firewood peddler. He was suddenly enlightened when he heard the *Diamond Sutra* being recited in the marketplace. He decided to join the Zen temple led by Hung-jen (601–674), the Fifth Patriarch, to learn more.

Despite his lack of education, Hui-neng showed exceptional intuitive understanding. Hung-jen asked his students to produce an enlightenment poem. The senior student, Shen-hsui (605–706) wrote,

Our body is the bodhi tree
And our mind a mirror bright
Carefully we wipe them now by hour
And let no dust alight.
(Price & Mau-Lam 1990, 70)

On hearing this poem, the master knew that Shen-hsui had not reached enlightenment. Zen is not just about trying to wipe away the dust of thoughts. Hui-neng, realizing this, composed his own poem:

There is no bodhi-tree
Nor stand of mirror bright
Since all is void,
Where can the dust alight?
(Price & Mau-Lam 1990, 72)

Hung-jen recognized the enlightened wisdom in this stanza and gave Hui-neng his robe and bowl as symbols of direct transmission. But because Hui-neng lacked the distinguished background of Shen-hsui, his senior student, the master told Hui-neng to leave and start his own temple, which he did.

Hui-neng became the dominant figure in the Zen lineage in China. He believed that the void is not a vacuum. The void is filled with the universe of things, people, and our entire world. He taught us to keep our minds detached without suppressing thinking. He advised: "We take idea-lessness as our object" (Price & Mou-lam 1990, 96). The mind is by nature pure, so by staying with the void in the midst of everything we live fully while remaining completely in tune with our original, true nature.

The T'ang Dynasty (618–907): Zen Evolves with Creative Masters

Zen grew during the T'ang period with many great masters teaching all around China. These masters were individualistic and eccentric. Their sincere commitment to Zen inspired not only the students they taught directly, but also future generations of students who would learn from accounts of their actions described in koans.

Ma-tzu (709–88) expressed Zen teachings with ardor and force. He shouted and taught with such sudden and eccentric behavior that students would experience a momentary gap in their ordinary consciousness that offered the potential for enlightenment.

One of Ma-tzu's students, Pai-chang (720–814), created rules for monastic life that included ethical vows, working, eating, and sleeping, along with meditation as part of Zen practice. These traditions are followed to this day. Huang-po (d. 850), next in the lineage, taught his students to rid themselves of everything, all concepts and beliefs, to discover the radiant clarity that is already present in the mind. He became the teacher of one of the most memorable Zen masters, Lin-chi (d. 866), founder of Rinzai, one of the two main schools of Zen.

Lin-chi, whose name translates as Rinzai in Japanese, encouraged his students to have faith in themselves, in their deepest nature. We are all people of no rank, he liked to say, and so if you remove all external labels and positions, you will see that nothing is actually missing! True rank cannot be taken away. True rank is our true nature.

Lin-chi also popularized the symbolic use of blows with a stick to bring about enlightenment. When students were suddenly struck for reasons beyond their limited grasp of meaning, they felt a compelling reaction to greater understanding. Lin-chi was an exceptional teacher who inspired many through his loud yells, sharp blows, and humanistic heart.

During the second half of the T'ang Dynasty, five different schools of Zen evolved, known as the Five Houses. They included the Lin-chi school, which became Rinzai Zen in Japan, and the T'sao-tung School, which later became Soto Zen in Japan.

Sung Dynasty Period (960–1279): Zen Expands

Zen became a prominent component of Chinese culture during the Sung period of renaissance in China. A state system for teaching Zen known as Five Mountains, Ten Temples trained large numbers of students. Koans were introduced to give the many students a feeling of direct transmission from the earlier T'ang masters. Japanese and Korean monks journeyed to China to learn Zen first hand and bring it back to their countries where Zen would experience new creative growth and development.

Korean Zen

Korea received Zen directly from students of Ma-tzu and other Chinese masters. These Korean students returned to their country and founded remote mountain temples, known as the Nine Mountain Schools. These schools functioned independently of State Buddhism; the monks grew their own food and took care of their own needs. The division between sudden enlightenment and Buddhist learning grew and evolved.

One of Korea's greatest masters was Chinul (1158–1210), a comprehensive thinker who helped to unify Zen with other forms of Buddhism in Korea. He believed in maintaining a constant effort to integrate sudden enlightenment into everyday life. This unifying of sudden awakening with gradual cultivation is still practiced today in many Korean monasteries.

Japanese Zen

Japan learned Zen from the Chinese, but the Japanese took Zen in new directions and enriched the practice for the world.

Eisai (1141–1215) is credited as the Japanese founder of Zen. He was the first to form a lasting Zen temple in Japan, called Kennin-ji monastery in Kyoto. Hoping to reform Japanese Buddhism, Eisai visited China and acquired a greater understanding from the sources. He brought Rinzai Zen back to Japan and struggled for acceptance against conservative Buddhist doctrines. Little did he know what a huge impact Zen would have as a school in its own right.

Dogen, Japan's Inspirational Soto Master

Dogen (1200–1253)—a student of Myozen, Eisai's disciple—brought Soto Zen to Japan. Dogen became one of Japan's greatest Zen teachers. He journeyed throughout China in search of broader training and met a great Soto teacher named Ju-ching (1163–1228), who had just become the new abbot at Ching-te-ssu. Dogen became Ju-ching's student and quickly attained enlightenment. Dogen learned that the quality of practice is most important. This is a primary principle of Soto Zen: Practice is not separate from enlightenment, practice is enlightenment. Thus everything you do in your life is an opportunity to practice Zen and to be enlightened. There is no separation.

With Ju-ching's approval, Dogen brought Soto back to Japan and taught his students to devote themselves to sitting in meditation, zazen, with absolute devotion. Dogen was the first Japanese monk to rely only on Zen and nothing else; he said it was essential to commit yourself to an ethical life by receiving the precepts, the Buddhist rules for conduct and moral code. He believed that if you live ethically and devote yourself to Zen meditation, nothing holds you back.

Zen Integrates into Japanese Culture

Dogen's Soto School spread through Japan, as did the Rinzai School originally founded by Eisai. The Japanese government established a system similar to the Five Mountains, Ten Temples system in China. In the Japanese system, an elaborate hierarchy of temples and sub-temples reached out from the cities into the most remote rural areas. Zen monks educated children in monastery schools and advised emperors and government leaders at every level.

The Zen Way is an approach to life that enhances every aspect of living. Zen arts—martial arts, calligraphy, tea ceremonies, flower arrangement, gardening, haiku, and archery, for example—developed as a pathway to follow for a living experience of the true spirit of Zen. Practitioners of these arts mastered Zen as they developed tremendous artistic skills, which you will explore later in this book.

Hakuin

One of Japan's most influential Rinzai Zen masters, Hakuin (1685–1768) led a tiny, run-down monastery in his hometown farming village of Hara, near the base of Mount Fuji. Despite his humble position, Hakuin had a lasting effect on Zen.

Hakuin pursued enlightenment with an unparalleled ardor. He encouraged his students to do the same, to strive for enlightenment like a person running from a burning building. He believed that nothing should interfere with your single-minded determination to penetrate into your own true nature. A single enlightenment was only the beginning in Hakuin's view. The Zen Path is a lifelong pursuit to be followed sincerely and passionately.

He believed that nothing could surpass meditation in the midst of activity. Although quietly sitting in meditation has its place, he felt it is far more important to sustain deep meditation no matter what you are doing:

> I am not trying to tell you to discard completely quietistic meditation and to seek specifically for a place of activity to carry on your practice. What is most worthy of respect is pure koan meditation that neither knows nor is conscious of the two aspects, the quiet and the active. (Hakuin in Yampolsky 1971, 15–16)

Hakuin and his disciples revitalized and organized koans into a progressive system of study to help guide students on their path. The first koan, Mu, was used to help students penetrate deeply into their true nature. He created the famous koan, "What is the sound of one hand clapping?" This organized course of study had a broad appeal to both monks and laymen by giving a definite pathway for Zen development.

Hakuin was also a prolific calligrapher and painter who created over 5000 works. Many of his pictures were amusing caricatures and poems with simple mottos, which he often generously gave to the townspeople who enjoyed them. He was beloved by the everyday person as well as the many Zen practitioners he taught. Hakuin's influence continues to be felt today. (See Hakuin's painting of Bodhidharma, Daruma in Japanese, on page 12.)

Zen in the West

Zen was largely unknown to the West until its introduction at the Worldwide Conference on Religion, a cross-cultural gathering in Chicago, in 1893. D.T. Suzuki (1870–1966) accompanied the Zen representative, Shaku Soen, as translator. Suzuki met an American publisher, Paul Carus (1852–1919), who brought Suzuki to America to translate a series of Eastern classics. This set Suzuki on a life-long path of writing and teaching Westerners about Zen Buddhism. His many books and years of teaching at Columbia University influenced the beatniks, modern artists, intellectuals, psychologists, and countless people who read his books.

Many other Zen masters came to America and Europe during the twentieth century, setting up Zen temples and teaching at universities. Most found Westerners to be avid learners who brought a fresh and open "beginner mind" spirit to Zen (S. Suzuki, 1979). Shunryu Suzuki, a quiet master of Soto Zen, founded the San Francisco Zen Center. Korean Master Seung Sahn formed a large organization of Korean Zen, Kwan-Um, that is actively growing in the United States and Europe. Thanks to these and many other Zen masters and their disciples, Zen continues to evolve as it meets with the new challenges of the twenty-first century.

Meditation

Tapping Mind's Potential

Zazen in Japanese consists of two characters, *za* and *zen*. If we
analyze the literal meanings of them, za means to sit cross-
legged, zen, to calmly concentrate one's mind. (Shibayama
1993, 78)

Taking the First Step on Your Zen Path

A scholar studied philosophy for many years. He knew a great deal about
the different types of philosophy, both Western and Eastern. He heard
about a great Zen master and decided to visit him. When he arrived, the Zen
master welcomed him in and said, "Please join me for tea." The scholar was
pleased, since he had heard about the significance of Zen tea ceremonies.

They sat down together and the master began preparing the tea. The
scholar thought he should tell the master about himself. He said, "I've been
studying philosophy for many years. I know about the various types of
Buddhism, such as Tendai, Shingon, and Zen. I've read Dogen and Hakuin
and I think I liked Hakuin better, although Dogen had a lot of good ideas
too. Well, they're both good, of course. . . ."

Daruma, Hakuin Etaku. Eighteenth century, Japan. Ink on paper, hanging scroll. Gift of Murray Smith, Los Angeles County Museum of Art.

The master continued preparing the tea without a word. The scholar said, "I wanted to ask you about the idea of emptiness. How does it relate to the philosophical concept of being and nonbeing?"

The master silently handed him a cup and began to pour.

The student continued on with his many thoughts about philosophy: "I have thought a lot about theories of being and nonbeing. I have read Aristotle, Plato, and the existentialists. Sartre had an interesting theory, and of course Camus dealt with it. I think. . . ."

The master kept pouring and pouring until the tea began spilling out.

Startled, the student said, "Master! My cup is overflowing!"

The master smiled and said simply, "As is your mind. How can I show you Zen if you don't first empty your cup?"

This classic story illustrates how to take the first steps on your path to learning Zen. Zen does not involve the accumulation of new knowledge and information. Zen helps you discover what and who you really are. Meditation is the method used to make these discoveries for yourself.

> Make your will one! Don't listen with your ears, listen with your mind. No, don't listen with your mind, but listen with your spirit. Listening stops with the ears, the mind stops with recognition, but spirit is empty and waits on all things. The Way gathers in emptiness alone. Emptiness is the fasting of the mind. (The Taoist sage, Chuang-tzu in Watson 1968, 58)

Zen finds meaning in emptiness. All things are empty, without form, in their true nature. The Taoists saw the significance of emptiness too when they said, "The usefulness in a cup is in its emptiness." Once you fill a cup, it can no longer be used. Thus, empty yourself and you will get to something useful, with infinite possibilities.

But emptying yourself is only half the truth. The *Heart Sutra* says, "Form is emptiness and emptiness is form." As you journey along the Zen Path, you fill your consciousness with questions, probing deeply.

Like a person lost in the desert searching for water, your single-minded resolve is to understand yourself and your world.

Your Zen journey empties your mind of problems and illusions so it can fill with new understanding. If you feel confused, that's a good beginning. Step on your path with confidence. As Lin Chi told his students, "When students today fail to make progress, where's the fault? The fault lies in the fact that they don't have faith in themselves!" (Watson 1993, 23).

What Is Meditation?

In Japanese, "Zen" translates as "meditation." Meditation is a time when you sit quietly, seemingly doing nothing. In Western cultures, sitting quietly and doing nothing might seem like a waste of time. How can anything significant be accomplished by doing nothing? Or are you really doing nothing? The answers to these questions require a shift in perspective. If you are willing to experiment with this shift, a whole new world of possibility opens up for you.

When you meditate, you take a break from all the usual thoughts and activities that fill your life. As you learn how to quiet your thoughts, you begin to perceive clearly in a new way. You become in touch with a deeper part of yourself. We are all endowed with a mind that is clear, pure, and deep. This is what the Zen masters call our true nature. It is already there, within everyone, but we usually don't notice because we are too busy being pushed and pulled by our thoughts and desires.

Meditation is a tool that teaches you how to return to your deeper experience to perceive clearly, resulting in a profound sense of calm and confidence that won't be shaken. As you get more accustomed to meditation, you realize that what seemed at first to be a non-activity is really its own kind of activity. Meditation lets you be immersed in your usual everyday life while also remaining fully aware.

The purpose is to see things as they are, to observe things as they are, and to let everything go as it goes. This is to put everything under control in its widest sense. (S. Suzuki, 1979, 33)

Meditation is the cornerstone of Zen. All ideas, writings, and actions are secondary to meditation. To truly know Zen, you must engage in meditation. Experiment with the meditations in this lesson and you will begin to know Zen for yourself.

Surmounting Difficulties in Meditation

Some people will find that meditation comes naturally to them, and others will have some difficulty. Don't judge your performance. If you have trouble, consider your difficulties challenges, like bumps on a road—You don't stop traveling because the road gets a little rough.

You may choose to visit one of the many Zen centers around the world, where a Zen master guides your meditation. At a center, you will learn meditation with others, which some people find easier.

If you are an independent sort of person, you may prefer to meditate on your own. Many great Zen masters found their enlightenment on their own. Anyone can be enlightened if they make the effort. Sense what is best for you; and most importantly, meditate!

Preparing for Meditation

Meditation can be done anywhere at any time, but when you first start, find a quiet, private, temperate place with subdued lighting. Pick a time when you don't have any immediate responsibilities. At first, devote a short amount of time to meditation, even as little as one minute. Eventually, as you begin to feel the benefits, you will probably feel more motivated to increase the time that you spend meditating.

Meditation Postures

There is a traditional way to sit on the floor in meditation, which is still followed today in many Zen temples. But don't let the conventions for positioning prevent you from meditation. If you can't sit on the floor, use a chair. Meditation comes from within, so don't let your body restrictions hold you back.

Position for Zazen
Place a pillow on the floor. Sit down and cross your legs into the lotus position where the left heel rests on the right thigh and the right heel rests on the left thigh. If you don't have the flexibility for this position, sit with only one foot up, known as a half lotus, or simply sit cross-legged with both feet resting on the floor.

Place your hands on your lap, with your left hand on top of your right, middle joints of your middle fingers together, and thumbs lightly touching. Your hands will be shaped like an oval. One reason for crossing your legs and hands is to make your body a unity, with no distinction between left and right, no beginning and no end.

Sit with your spine straight, aligning your head in the center without tilting. Relax your shoulders and keep your head straight. Don't strain. Your breathing passages should be free and unrestricted. Let your breathing be normal.

Keep your eyes half open. (Traditionally, eyes were not entirely shut to prevent the monks from falling asleep.) Remain relaxed, but alert.

Warming Up to Meditation
You may benefit from exercises that teach how to deliberately sit still, relax, and direct attention. If you have never done anything like meditation before, work with your inner mind a bit to get accustomed to this new form of consciousness. The following three preliminary exercises help build useful skills for Zen meditation:

Warm Up 1: Just Sitting
Sitting quietly and doing nothing may be a challenge for some people, especially those who are accustomed to always being on the go. But taking some time to sit quietly is very helpful for learning Zen (and for a calmer life in general). Try this for a few minutes when you aren't busy:

Sit in a comfortable place, alone with yourself. Don't think about anything in particular, but don't try to stop thinking, either. Just sit quietly, breathing normally. You will probably notice that your mental activity slows somewhat as you sit. You may find yourself becoming more relaxed. After sitting for a few minutes, return to your normal activity. Try doing this exercise at various times during your day. You may be surprised to discover that just sitting can be beneficial.

Warm Up 2: Mindful Relaxation
We can all benefit from learning how to relax. Lie on your back on a wooden floor or on a carpet. Place your feet flat on the floor, knees raised to allow your back to relax naturally. Breathe comfortably.

Turn your attention to your body. People commonly hold tension in their necks, shoulders, or backs. Start at your head and scan down through your body. Notice any tension. As you continue to breathe gently, let go of unnecessary tensions. Don't force anything, just become aware of what you feel. This may take a few minutes. Continue to become aware of your body and allow relaxation wherever possible. Becoming aware of yourself, just as you are, is the essence of Zen.

Warm Up 3: Counting the Breaths Concentration
Mindful breathing helps the meditator experience the "here-and-now" and can be a natural inroad into meditation. Sit quietly and pay attention to your natural breathing. Inhale and exhale, counting each complete breath. Count ten breaths and then begin again. Let your breathing be relaxed. Remember to concentrate on your breathing as you continue counting for several minutes.

Zen Meditations

Now that you are more accustomed to working with your awareness and inward focus, you will enjoy beginning your Zen meditation. Even though enlightenment seems like the goal, Zen is goalless. You must let go of the desire to attain that goal, while at the same time trying very hard to keep meditating. This probably seems like a contradiction: to try without trying, to have a goal without striving. But it makes perfect sense from an enlightened perspective.

Dogen often told his students that practice is enlightenment. Life is not preparation for something else, the preparation is life itself, and here is where you will find enlightenment. When you truly appreciate each moment and stay fully aware, you will know Zen. These classic meditations will guide you on this well-worn path:

Meditation 1: Attention to Breathing
Sit in the traditional posture described earlier and relax your breathing. Direct your attention to your breathing. As you inhale, notice how your ribcage expands slightly as you bring air in and down through your breathing passages. Pay attention as the air pushes out again. Keep your awareness on each new breath, in and then out, as you allow the process to happen naturally. If any thoughts distract you, gently bring your attention back to your breathing. Let yourself experience each breath anew, as a fresh moment. Continue staying with your moment-by-moment breathing.

Meditation 2: Traditional Zazen
One of the great traditions in meditation, zazen, clears the mind. But clearing the mind is not like wiping every speck of dust off a mirror. Zen teaches you how to let go of distractions that interfere with your clear awareness, as this famous story illustrates:

A Zen student was trying very hard to make his mind clear like a mirror. He sat quietly and tried to think of nothing. But thoughts inevitably kept distracting him. Feeling in despair he asked his master, "No matter how hard I try, I cannot clear my mind! What should I do?"

The master picked up a tile that was on the ground and began polishing it with his robe. Confused, the student asked, "Master, what are you doing?"

"I am polishing this tile to make it into a mirror."

"That's impossible! You cannot make a tile into a mirror," said the student.

The master smiled. "Nor can you make your mind into a mirror!"

Meditation helps you experience what is already there. You don't have to change the mind you have or add anything new. Think of your mind as a murky lake that becomes clear when the mud settles to the bottom. The potential for clarity is there in the lake, but the sediment is stirred up. All you need to do is allow everything to settle.

Sit quietly and try not to think about anything. Stay with each moment, without adding any thoughts. Inevitably, thoughts will crop up. As a thought occurs, notice it but let it go. Then return to thinking of nothing. Continue to notice any thoughts that come up, but try not to get involved in them. As soon as you can, return yourself to no thought. Eventually your thoughts will slow down, leaving you with a clear, calm consciousness.

Meditation 3: Mindful Meditation
Consider the following story:

A Zen student had been studying for a number of years. An accomplished master, he was about to be recognized for his achievement and promoted to teacher. One rainy day before his promotion, he visited his first Zen teacher, whom he hadn't seen in a long time. Before he entered, he respectfully left his shoes and umbrella outside the door and continued barefooted. He bowed to his instructor and said a warm hello. His instructor was visibly glad to see him.

The instructor asked, "Tell me, which side of the door did you leave your shoes and umbrella?" The student thought for a moment and then bowed his head in shame. He had been so excited to see his old teacher that his anticipation had interfered with his mindful awareness of where he placed his shoes and umbrella. He decided to postpone his promotion and go back to his meditation because he had experienced a lapse in his awareness. Until he could sustain his awareness no matter what the circumstances he was not ready to teach. Eventually he did become a true master, mindfully aware in whatever he did.

With this story as inspiration, try this meditation: Sit quietly and experience the present moment. Keep your awareness on each new moment. Notice whatever you are experiencing, but try not to get lost in one thought and lose touch with the present. If you feel your awareness moving away from the present, gently bring it back. Keep being aware with each new moment.

Meditation 4: Slow Walking
Traditionally, Zen monks interspersed their long day of sitting meditation with walking meditation. Using the mindful meditation from the previous exercise, stand up and walk slowly. Hold your hands together in the position used for Zen meditation. Pay attention to how your foot meets the ground with every step. Notice how your weight shifts from foot to foot. Keep your breathing and your body relaxed as you walk slowly, and maintain your mindful awareness of every step.

Meditation 5: Fast Walking
When you are comfortable with the slow walking meditation, try fast walking. The monks used this meditation for exercise. Fast walking can be vigorous, stimulating, and challenging.

Allow your arms to hang at your sides and move freely as you walk. Take long strides and move quickly. Even though you are moving fast, maintain full awareness of every step. Be aware of weight shifts, how your foot meets the ground, how your body naturally coordinates with the movements. Stay fully focused on the moment-to-moment experience with a clear mind.

Meditation 6: Searching for Your True Nature

This meditation is drawn directly from Hakuin. Think carefully about the following passage:

> A student asked Hakuin, "What can I do to become awakened to my own mind?" Hakuin answered with a series of questions: "What is it that asks the question? Is it your mind? Is it your original nature? Is it some kind of spirit or demon? Is it inside you? Outside you? Is it somewhere in between? Is it blue, yellow, red, or white?" (Waddell 1994, 61)

Hakuin advises to keep thinking about "it" with single-minded devotion no matter what you are doing. So reflect upon these questions deeply, relying only on yourself. The answers can only be found within.

Sutras

Initiating a Zen
Perspective

A special tradition outside the scriptures
No dependence upon words or letters
Direct pointing at the soul of man
Seeing into one's nature and the attainment of buddhahood.
(Bodhidharma in Simpkins & Simpkins 1996, 21)

Bodhidharma set the foundation for Zen as a transmission beyond words. But words are not useless to Zen. Words point in a certain direction and awaken experiences within.

Sutras are the written words of Buddhist tradition that convey Buddhist ideas and point to the experience of enlightenment. Many schools of Buddhism study the sutras carefully to deepen their understanding using the intellect. But when used in the Zen way, sutras can be helpful as an opportunity to orient the mind. Traditional sutras offer meditations and topics to ponder, to be used as springboards to your own understandings. Look beyond the words and classical doctrine; find meaning that inspires you and points to your own inner realization.

Sutras are multi-layered and open to numerous interpretations. Please consider possibilities other than the ones presented here. Open your mind and heart and make discoveries.

Although the spirit of each sutra is summarized below, you may want to read the complete sutra for yourself. You can find English translations of all the sutras included here. Use our bibliography as a resource. The Internet also offers translations with comments from contemporary practitioners.

Vimalakirti Sutra

The *Vimalakirti Sutra* introduces the idea that anyone can be enlightened. Vimalakirti was a layman who was also a highly enlightened Buddhist. He lived an ordinary life, ran a business, owned a house, and had a family. At the same time, he had deep Buddhist insight. Whatever Vimalakirti did in his life, he used it as an opportunity to live and teach Buddhism: "Although he ate and drank (like others) he delighted in tasting the flavor of meditation" (Luk 1972, 16).

The sutra illustrates Vimalakirti's deep wisdom by favorably comparing him to Buddha's most famous disciples. In this way, the sutra gives hope to people from all walks of life that they too can be just as wise as the most enlightened Buddhists.

Reflection on Potential
You too can become enlightened. Think about your potential for inner wisdom and compassionate action. You may not be that way now, but entertain the idea that if you truly commit yourself, you could make it happen.

Meditation in Action
When Vimalakirti became ill, Buddha sent his disciples to visit Vimalakirti's bedside. One by one they hesitated because they felt inferior to Vimalakirti's level of insight. Each one explained what he

learned from Vimalakirti in the past. These discussions contain lessons in Buddhism for the reader.

For example, one disciple, Sariputra, recounted how Vimalakirti once taught him that meditation is not just a sedentary activity to be performed in seclusion. He taught him that every endeavor is an opportunity to meditate. One need not cut off activities or emotions if one maintains a meditative mind. He encouraged Sariputra to integrate meditation into everything he did.

Meditation while Doing

As you become more adept at meditating, extend your meditations beyond quietly sitting alone. Can you meditate while going about your daily life?

No Material Obstructions to Enlightenment

Finally, Sariputra reluctantly visited Vimalakirti's bedside. When he arrived, he was surprised to see a tiny room with no extra space for visitors. He asked Vimalakirti, "Where can I possibly sit?" Vimalakirti answered, "Did you come here for a seat or for the Dharma [Buddhist teachings]?" Here, Vimalakirti explained to Sariputra that Buddhist teachings are not found in the material world. Once Sariputra understood, an enormous room appeared, filled with thrones and people. Vimalakirti said, "This small room can contain these high and large thrones which do not obstruct anything because liberation makes everything possible" (Luk 1972, 65).

One of the important themes in the *Vimalakirti Sutra* is that it doesn't matter how things appear—You don't have to live in a perfect environment to be happy and enlightened. What is really important is how you think and feel as well as what you do. You can have the beauty of enlightenment in the midst of your life, even though it may be complicated or imperfect.

Contemplation on Environment

Think about your own life-situation. Do you tend to judge it nega-
tively? Do you think you cannot be enlightened in your own life?
Consider the lotus flower. This beautiful flower does not grow on an
isolated hillside; instead the lotus is found in the middle of a muddy
marsh. How does this relate to your personal situation?

Remember that Zen encourages us to let go of judgments, for they
sometimes lead us away from the positive possibilities in things.
Experiment with a more neutral attitude. Start where you are, whatever the circumstance.

How Do You Enter the Zen Path?

When all the monks had gathered around Vimalakirti, Manjusri, the
Bodhisattva of compassion, asked everyone how a person should be
initiated into the dharma. Everyone offered an opinion, some theoretical, others religious or philosophical. Vimalakirti answered with
silence. Manjusri said to him, "Excellent, excellent. Can there be true
initiation into the non-dual dharma until words and speech are no
longer written or spoken?"

An important message of this sutra is to be yourself as you maintain meditative awareness. Meditation is done without words; it's a
direct experience. Enlightened wisdom is unknowable.

Vimalakirti Sutra's Lesson

Zen is not something theoretical, complicated, or in any way beyond
you. It is found in the silent action of being kind and doing good in
the world. Everyday life, in each moment of day-to-day living, is a
spiritual experience. The two are not separate so you don't have to
seek a separate place outside of your regular life to find Zen enlightenment.

Lankavatara Sutra

> The waves of the mind ocean are stirred uninterruptedly by the wind of objectivity. (*Lankavatara Sutra* in Suzuki 1973, 40)

The *Lankavatara Sutra* holds an important place in Zen because it was Bodhidharma's favorite. According to legend, Bodhidharma gave this sutra to his disciple Hui-k'o, telling him that the *Lankavatara* was the only sutra he would ever need. Indeed, it contains all the basic themes of Mahayana Buddhism. It also uniquely describes consciousness and awareness, showing how the mind creates its problems and how the mind therefore overcomes them.

Importance of Self Realization

The *Lankavatara Sutra* stresses the idea that Zen must be an inner experience. Even though teachers and books may guide you along the way, no one can give you enlightenment; you must discover it for yourself. The sutra promises to lead people in the right direction: "...ask and I will instruct you concerning of the inmost realization" (*Lankavatara Sutra* trans. by Suzuki 1957, 65).

The Use of Words

If you let a sutra's words guide you, it is important to recognize the difference between words and their meaning. Words are like a searchlight, helping to illuminate your path in the dark. The light has no reality of its own; rather, words illuminate through their meaning, which resonates within you. Enlightenment cannot be expressed by language. Words are merely lines and circles on a page. Don't mistake the finger pointing to the moon for the moon itself. True understanding of Zen must always return to wordless experience: "By means of the lamp and discrimination, the Bodhisattva-Mahasattvas go beyond word and discrimination and enter upon the path of self-realization" (*Lankavatara Sutra* trans. by Suzuki 1957, 109).

Mind-Only Is the Measure of All Things

What then is self-realization? The *Lankavatara Sutra* points to mind-only. Nothing in the world, including ideas, things, and even our self is real even though they all seem very real. Everything actually comes from the mind.

The *Lankavatara Sutra* explains how our illusions of reality and permanence come about. To fully understand mind-only, people undergo a change in consciousness. Similar to recognizing that the water that appears on a hot sunny road is only a mirage, not really there, so people come to understand that everything, including social and cultural experience, is only a construction of mind. On the other hand, the mirage-like world is there for the fleeting moment it is perceived, and so it does have reality.

This is where meditation is useful as a method that can access mental processing of pure intuition, beyond logic and reason. When you observe the world from the perspective of pure consciousness, beyond words, you have a glimpse of mind-only.

Experiencing Manifestations of Mind

Everything in our world takes on a certain reality because of the mind that experiences it. Follow this logic for a first-hand glimpse of this idea:

Your own home has a certain meaning to you as the place where you live. But your perception of your home has probably changed over time. Recall the first time you entered your home, how it seemed to you then. Compare this memory to how you experience it now, filled with the possessions, memories, and experiences you have had there. It probably seems very different to you now. Contemplate how your perspective affects your experiencing.

Theory of Consciousness

The *Lankavatara Sutra* explores consciousness to help understand mind-only. Consciousness is divided into eight levels, which the sutra calls *vijnanas*. The first five are consciousness through the five senses. For example, vision is not just the eyes seeing, but also the mind seeing.

The idea of the mind seeing corresponds well with what modern psychology has discovered. Sensing is a cognitive process combining eyes, brain, and mind. Thus, an individual who has perfect eyes may be blind if the visual cortex in the brain is damaged. We see through the eyes, not only with the eyes. Or we may avoid seeing things in plain view that we find disturbing. Our perceptions are not just like seeing with a camera because our mind is always interacting with our eyes and processing the information from the senses. The Buddhists call this eye-vijnana, eye consciousness. All of the five senses also have consciousness. The sutra adds a sixth vijnana corresponding to the intellect.

These six vijnanas deceive us about the true nature of the world. The sutra uses an analogy of a dark blue ocean. Ocean water is not blue, yet we see a blue ocean and think of oceans as blue. This is but one example of how the vijnanas mislead us. Our lives are permeated with such misconceptions that lead us away from true understanding.

The seventh vijnana, Manas, is where illusionary thinking originates. We create the idea of self and a permanent, real world. We make distinctions the sutra calls discriminations, between ourselves and others, good and bad, this and that. Manas is the source: "For instance, Mahamati, space cannot be numbered, and it is due to our discrimination that it is designated as such" (*Lankavatara Sutra* in Suzuki 1973, 108).

The eighth vijnana, Alaya, is pure awareness, awareness without thought, without an object or any meaningful intention toward an object. You get a glimpse of such consciousness spontaneously when something falls off a shelf and you reach out to catch it, without thought. Truly moving, life-altering experiences are also encounters with Alaya.

We live better and happier when we experience life directly without the mediation of our usual modes of categorizing and reasoning. Pure awareness is not only possible but also superior. It is our original nature that is capable of just being and doing—naturally, whole-heartedly, with nothing standing in the way.

This then, is what the sutra means by "everything is mind-only." Your journey into Zen is your own first hand experience of mind-only. Once you discover pure, objectless, choiceless awareness, a compassionate heart is awakened. Suzuki believes that this awakening of the compassionate heart is the most important idea in the sutra and in all Buddhism.

Prajnaparamita, Perfect Wisdom Sutras

A large collection of shorter works, the *Prajnaparamita Sutras* carefully explain the compassionate lifestyle that complements the enlightened consciousness that the *Lankavatara* describes.

"Prajnaparamita" translates as "Perfect Wisdom." "Prajna" means wisdom and "paramita" means getting to the other shore, or "to get beyond knowing things to pure knowing" (Low 2000, 31). So these sutras do not offer facts and information to be memorized and categorized. They state repeatedly that they offer nothing. Instead, readers are led to think differently. Such a complete turnaround in consciousness brings about enlightenment and the relief of suffering.

Two of the later *Prajnaparamita Sutras* have become cornerstones to Zen practice: The *Diamond Sutra* and the *Heart Sutra*. We encourage you to read both of these sutras. They are very accessible with numerous English translations available.

Diamond Sutra

So you should view all of the fleeting world:
A star at dawn, a bubble in the stream;

A flash of lightning in a summer cloud;
A flickering lamp, a phantom, and a dream.
(From the last chapter of the Diamond Sutra in
Mu Soeng 2000, 155)

Diamonds are the hardest element that can cut through other substances, even ones that are dense and difficult to cut. The name of this sutra, *Diamond Sutra*, also known as the *Diamond Cutter Sutra*, indicates the purpose of this work: to cut through the many illusions people have about the nature of the self and the world. When illusion is cut away, what remains is direct perception and clear experience of enlightenment.

The *Diamond Sutra* is a question and answer conversation between Buddha and his disciple Subhuti. Through very paradoxical dialogue, Buddha leads Subhuti and the reader to a change in perspective, a different consciousness. Subhuti asks Buddha what seekers of awakening should rely on and what should they do to master their thinking. The answer lies at the crux of Zen and is the subject of the *Diamond Sutra*. Once you perceive as the sutra suggests, you will be well on your Way.

Emptiness

One by one, the sutra dispenses with usual, taken-for-granted ideas. Buddha explains that everything in our world—including animals, plants, and even rocks—is made up of the same stuff. Human beings think they themselves are special, but the human "self," in its essence, is no different from anything else in the world. Everything, including people, is made up of aggregates of qualities that are ultimately empty in their true nature. And so, Buddha teaches, we should have compassion toward others, as well as the objects and creatures of the world. We all share the same nature.

This quality of emptiness is a fundamental idea in Zen. Emptiness is similar to bamboo, which has form on the outside but is hollow or empty on the inside. Thus the significance of bamboo in many Zen paintings is to represent this primary theme of emptiness.

Modern physics has come to a similar understanding. Matter is not solid like our senses tell us, but is actually comprised of energy. Even though things aren't really solid we continue to experience them that way.

This same logic applies to our personal self. We hold our feelings of self to be real and enduring. But the Diamond Sutra clearly states that in reality the "self" does not exist. The self is merely a collection of traits that in their true essence are empty just like everything else. And so we should have compassion toward others, as well as the objects and creatures of the world. We all share the same nature.

Emptiness Contemplation
Think about the Zen idea that everything is empty. Consider this in regard to yourself. You know that you are real, of course, but you are more than just a definition or concept of yourself. You are always growing, always changing. Learning to have a flexible self-concept is a hallmark of a healthy personality. Zen goes further—let go of your self-concept and simply be at one with others, unique each moment.

Paradox
The *Diamond Sutra* can be difficult to understand at first partly because it expresses seemingly contradictory ideas. One typical example:

> Subhuti asked the Buddha, "World-Honored One, is the highest, most fulfilled, awakened mind that the Buddha attained the unattainable?"

> The Buddha said, "That is right Subhuti. Regarding the most fulfilled, awakened mind, I have not attained anything. That is why it is called the highest, most fulfilled, awakened mind." (Hanh 1992, 20)

We in the West, schooled in Aristotelian logic, assume that things either exist or they don't exist. Something is either true or false. It is considered murky thinking to not know the difference. Perception sharpens by organizing information accurately. Contradictions can be resolved by this method. Or so we think.

Diamond Sutra's Lesson

The *Diamond Sutra* and other *Prajnaparamita Sutras* do not resolve contradiction: they embrace it. Perfect wisdom is found when you understand that things both exist and don't exist at the same time: a thing is and is not. Accepting such seemingly incompatible ideas stimulates a different consciousness, a wisdom known as prajna. But this wisdom is no wisdom, empty. When you embrace the *Diamond Sutra*, your perspective shifts.

The Heart Sutra: The Heart of Wisdom

The *Heart Sutra* consists of a few dozen lines that were pared down from a larger work to express the core teachings, and so it is often considered the heart or essence of wisdom. Most of the lines describe the nature of prajna wisdom, but the name also refers to the other side of wisdom: compassion. The *Heart Sutra* makes it clear that wisdom without compassion is not true wisdom. The *Heart Sutra* shows us that Zen is not a selfish practice. Everything and everyone is one unity, so if you hurt, I hurt. Therefore compassion is the appropriate and natural response for the Zen practitioner.

The *Heart Sutra* follows the same logic as the *Diamond Sutra*: there is nothing—no form, no consciousness, no attainment, no pain, no suffering, no body, no emotions, no birth, no death—nothing. Prajna wisdom is this realization on a deep level, taking a perspective that is no perspective.

One of the key lines of the *Heart Sutra* reads, "Know then: Form here is only emptiness, emptiness only form. Form is no other than emptiness, emptiness no other than form" (Low 2000, 35). The sutra states that emptiness is the true nature of everything, but that is only a partial understanding.

Emptiness is not equivalent or equal to form. One metaphor that may be helpful is a mirror and its reflection. Imagine emptiness as a mirror, and forms are reflections. Reflections depend on a mirror to reflect them, but they aren't literally the mirror itself. And no matter what is reflected or how much the reflections may change, the mirror never changes in what it is in itself. The true nature of form is emptiness because emptiness is like mind's mirror that reflects forms, creating them in the interaction.

Heart Sutra's Lesson

The *Heart Sutra* ends with a mantra, a group of words that are repeated over and over: *Gate, gate, paragate, parasamagate bodhi, sva-ha!* This translates as "gone, gone beyond, gone right beyond, how wonderful!" By going beyond all perspectives, beyond all wisdom, therein lies the heart of the *Heart Sutra*.

Meditation on Form Is Emptiness, Emptiness Is Form

The phrase "form is emptiness and emptiness is form" is also used as a mantra that is chanted in many Zen centers. Sit in a meditation position and say or think this line to yourself: "Form is emptiness and emptiness is form." As you do, relax and direct your attention to the phrase. Think about what these words really mean. What is the significance? After you have contemplated for some time, let go of any thoughts about it. With nothing in mind, simply sit quietly without thought. Breathe comfortably and stay with your moment-by-moment experience.

Avatamsaka (Hua-Yen) Sutras

The *Avatamsaka Sutras* are a large group of works gathered around the fourth century. A school of Buddhism developed from these teachings called the Hua-Yen in China or Kegon School in Japan. This sutra expresses an important theme of Zen: Unity.

"Avatamsaka" means wreath or garland, symbolizing unity in plurality. Each speck of dust contains the entire universe and the entire universe is contained in one speck of dust. There is no hierarchy where anything is more important or better than anything else, as we assume in the West. All is One and One is all.

This idea is expressed very beautifully in the sutra as the metaphorical image of Empress Indra's net. The net stretches all around Indra's palace. The net is made of precious pearls, all strung together and each reflecting all the others. When you pick up one pearl, you see all the others reflected in the one.

The world comes into being as we experience it in this moment of time. This idea, expressed in the *Avatamsaka Sutra*, is called "dependent co-origination." Things coexist in a flash of interrelationship at this moment.

The third patriarch of Hua-yen, named Fa-tsang (643–712), demonstrated co-dependent origination to the Empress Wu, who was studying Buddhism under him. He covered the entire floor, walls, and ceiling of a room in the palace with mirrors. Then he placed a statue of Buddha with a torch in the center. The moment the torch was lit, the Empress saw infinite Buddhas all at once, each reflecting all the others. This image gave her a powerful experience of unity. Everything came into being at a single moment, existing together just as it was. After she saw this demonstration, the Empress felt a deep understanding of what her teacher was trying to communicate.

Avatamsaka Sutra's Lesson

The idea that things are separate in their true nature is an illusion created by the mind. From one perspective, things are unique and separate, but from a wider perspective, this is only one aspect of an all-encompassing unity.

Meditation on All in One, All at Once

Sit comfortably and close your eyes. Take a few minutes to relax and center yourself in the present moment, then imagine Indra's net or Fa-tsang's mirrors. Let the image speak for itself. Don't analyze it. Just experience it.

Beyond the Sutras

Sutras are like a boat that takes you across the river, but once on shore, you must get off. Sutras carry you to the shore and invite you to experience enlightenment, but the process of exploration is your own. As you contemplate the different sutras, you open your mind to thinking in the Zen way. Use these ideas as springboards to your own experience, to awaken to your deeper nature. Then, go beyond them.

Koans

How to Think
Intuitively

Goso said, "When you meet a man of the Way on the way, do
not greet him with words, do not greet him with silence. Tell me
how will you greet him?"

(Case 36, *Mumonkan* in Low 1995, 219)

The brilliant pioneering masters of Zen taught with spontaneity and
creativity. These masters were unique individuals. They created situations for their students to learn from by their dialogues and everyday
circumstances. They drew from their own spontaneous interactions.
The seeds of Zen sprouted and grew in their students, and then finally
blossomed as Zen evolved. Some seeds were planted in distant lands,
some in remote mountain temples, others in the fertile soil of the
countryside. And as each of the lines of Zen grew, methods of cultivating the Zen experience evolved.

One method of transmitting Zen was through *koans*, which mean
"public record." The public records used in Zen were the stories,
words, and actions of the early Zen masters. As the number of koans

grew, they were gathered and used for the instruction, testing, and communication of wisdom.

Since Zen's doctrine, according to Bodhidharma, is direct pointing to the essence of reality, which is the source of words or even letters, Zen's literature and methods had to be consistent with that criterion. The cryptic, puzzling koan solved the problem posed by Bodhidharma and in turn, each koan poses a new problem to point the student's mind toward a deeper understanding.

Western thought is based in reason. We learn early in school to induce consequences from either/or, the Aristotelian logic of being vs. nonbeing: either something is or it is not. The sutras guide you toward a non-Aristotelian way of thinking, but even the sutras are only the scaffolding, not the understanding itself. A higher synthesis can be found through seeing into the true nature of the world. From this perspective, the dilemma is transcended.

Faith

Why should we struggle to understand something that seems to make no sense, like koans? Zen masters ask us to put our faith in the process and jump in with both feet. But not faith as we usually think of it. In the West, we often think of placing our faith in what is. But faith must be placed in not being: What is, actually is not. Faith is based in a paradox.

Things constantly change, going from birth to death. Placing our faith in finite being is always bound to lead to disappointment. But if we put our faith in what is not, we leave room for infinite possibility. The Taoists used the analogy of an uncarved block of wood. Before a block of wood is carved, it can be anything. The uncarved block has infinite possibility and yet it is nothing, just a block of wood. But once it is carved, for example, into a toy boat, we see only the boat. The toy goes through a life cycle and eventually falls apart: becomes unrecognizable as a boat and goes back to being just wood.

So, paradoxically, we must put our faith in what we are not, to become what we are and what we may become. This requires a new perspective. Koans direct us through the unknown, beyond being, toward a faith in positive potential.

The Evolution of Koans

According to Dumoulin, a prominent historian of Zen, the first documented use of koans was by Nan-yuan Hui-yung (d. 930), a student of the Lin Chi (Rinzai) School. Nan-yuan guided his students with enigmatic stories about how the T'ang masters fostered enlightenment with a word or an action. Gradually these accounts were gathered together and organized. The *Rinzairoku*, the renowned writings of Lin Chi, included many of these stories. Later, numerous koans were recorded, numbering up to 1700.

There were fewer followers when Zen evolved during the T'ang period. Spontaneous lessons from the masters could be transmitted directly from teacher to student. But during the Sung period (960–1279), many students flocked to Zen centers, and so koans were used extensively for teaching and testing levels of understanding. Koans were incorporated into writings, along with lectures, anecdotes, and sayings of the masters.

Two collections of koans are considered the most important: *The Blue Cliff Record (Hekiganroku)* and *The Gateless Gate (Mumonkan)*.

The *Hekiganroku* was originally collected by Setcho (980–1052), a great Zen master and poet. He added a poem to each koan, called the main subject. Nearly a century later, around 1128, Engo (Yuan-Wu Ko Chin 1063–1135) edited and collected Setcho's work and added extensive commentaries. He was a follower of the Lin Chi School and was also familiar with Confucian philosophy, so he presented koan concepts with structure. The work brought together one hundred koans into one book. But his disciple Ta-hui felt the commentaries were too revealing and destroyed the original book.

The collection was later recovered by a monk in 1300, who gathered together all surviving material as he best could. This book offered a systematic pattern of koan and commentary that became famous during the Sung Period. Modern translations tend to keep the introduction, main subject, and poem only. Some translators have added their own commentaries, while attempting to stay with the original meanings as much as possible.

Each koan is titled, followed by an introduction from Engo, which prepares the reader indirectly for the koan with hints of attitudes or emphasis. For example, the first case (koans are often referred to as cases), "Emperor Wu asks Bodhidharma" is about Bodhidharma's encounter with Emperor Wu when he first arrived in China after his long voyage from India. Emperor Wu, a devoted Buddhist, had heard about a monk who was absolutely devoted to meditation and wanted to talk with him.

Engo's introduction begins, "Smoke over the hill indicates fire, horns over the fence indicate an ox. Given one corner, you grasp the other three" (Sekida 1977, 147). This metaphor is drawn from Confucius, who stated that a bright student needs only a corner, one part of something to be learned to be able to grasp the rest (Simpkins & Simpkins 2000). Similarly, Engo tells students that these koans will require them to think far beyond what is given, to stretch their minds toward the whole.

The main subject is next and states the koan itself, beginning with:

> "What is the principle of Buddhism?"
> "Nothing."
> "Who is standing before me?"
> "No One."

Setcho's poem follows:

> The holy teaching? "Emptiness!"
> What is the secret here?
> Again, "Who stands before me?"
> "No knowing!"
> (Sekida, 1977, 147)

The *Mumonkan*, the second major koan collection, followed about one hundred years later. Composed by Master Mumon (Wu-Man 1183–1260), it contained forty-eight cases or koans, each chosen to help guide monks according to their different talents and personalities. In his introduction, Mumon asked students to devote themselves wholeheartedly, without holding back: "If you are brave you will dive right in without being worried about the risk. . . . However, if you hesitate, you will be like someone watching a horse gallop by the window. In a twinkling of an eye it has already gone" (Low 1995, 21).

Mumon did not organize the koans in a systematic way, although the first one is noteworthy, being one he had personally wrestled with for six long years. It is called "Joshu's (Chao-Chou) Mu," and Mumon never forgot the important effort he had undergone pondering this koan.

The koan states: A monk once asked Joshu, "Does a dog have Buddha Nature?" Joshu answered, "Mu."

The koan is followed by the author's comment. Mumon explains that Mu is the main gateway of Zen and that if you pass through it, you will see Joshu face-to-face. Passing through the gateway of the Mu koan is an important entry into Zen.

Mumon explained that Mu is not "nothing" nor is it relative: "Cast away your illusory discriminating knowledge and consciousness accumulated up until now, and keep on working harder" (Mumon in Loori 1994, 66). He urges the reader to concentrate on Mu with every ounce of energy. If you do this successfully, you will know how to work on all koans and you will be enlightened.

A verse composed by Mumon follows:

The dog! Buddha Nature!
The perfect manifestation, the command of truth.
If for a moment you fall into relativity,
You are dead as a doornail.
(Low 1995, 26)

Most modern translations include an additional commentary from the translator, which varies from translation to translation. They typically explain that Mu goes to the heart of existence. If you reduce everything that you know and are to Mu, what is Mu?

Rinzai and Soto:
Different Uses of Koans

Engo's successor, Ta-hui, refined koan practice, integrating it deeply into how Rinzai practitioners do Zen. Another contemporary school, The Ts'ao-tung School (Soto in Japan), took issue with koan use. They considered zazen more important. Dogen, the founder of Soto in Japan, believed that everything in life could be a koan. In this way, students could use any or all of their own moment-to-moment experience as a koan topic for meditation. Rinzai masters used specific stories and teaching dialogues culled from incidents with the earlier masters, shaping and developing them into koans, using them extensively to elicit the Zen experience of seeing into one's own true nature and then enlarging on that.

This difference between classical Soto and Rinzai has continued to some extent into modern times. Soto emphasizes zazen, sitting in meditation, to develop and enhance enlightened functioning. Therefore, Soto Zen teachers view koan analysis as distracting unless it helps to focus the mind. But this does not mean that focusing the mind cannot be accomplished with a koan as well. Since Dogen believed that everything in life could be viewed as a koan, the best place to begin is with your moment-by-moment ordinary experience. Perhaps the definition of a koan should not be so narrow and restricted.

Rinzai, while using deep introspection into a koan as a method, continually reminds students that koan study is not an invitation to analyze rationally. Rinzai students also stay with their moment-by-moment experience as the inroad to understanding. So the differences are not as sharp as they might seem.

Today, koans are used for various purposes in Soto, Rinzai, and in eclectic systems that continue and include both in their tradition. Koans serve as an object of meditation to communicate Zen transmission of mind. Filling the mind with a koan is one way to empty the mind; as Suzuki pointed out, koans can be used to so intensely occupy the attention that nothing else can be thought.

The private meeting between teacher and student, known as *dokusan*, is a contemporary method sometimes used along with koan study. Students are given a koan to work on. Periodically they meet with the master to communicate about the koan. The master invites a shift of perspective toward enlightenment in the student's mind.

Despite different uses of koans throughout all Zen, the principles are consistent and omnipresent: True nature is true nature.

Hakuin's Koan Groups

Hakuin organized koans into groups and categories, using them to systematically guide students toward enhancing enlightenment. He created five groups: Hossin, Kikan, Gonsen, Nanto, and Goi, with certain koans for each group. Following these are five more levels, called the Five Ranks.

The first three groups—Hossin, Kikan, and Gonsen—give a sense of how koans develop. The more esoteric koans in the later groups are usually learned with the guidance of a master, so we do not describe them here.

Hossin Koans

"Hossin" is the Japanese word for Dharmakaya. Dharmakaya is an important idea in Buddhism, explained by Lin Chi: "The pure light in each instant of thought is the Dharmakaya Buddha within your own house" (Miura & Sasaki 1965, 48). The Hossin koans begin the student's journey into understanding.

Here are two examples of these koans. You may choose to meditate on one of them: "When the cows of Eshu are well fed with grain, the horses of Ekishu have full stomachs." Or substitute familiar geographic areas: "When the cows of Ohio are well fed with grain, the horses of Montana have full stomachs."

This statement seems impossible. But from the perspective of unity, how are the cows and horses linked?

A student asked the master, "What is the pure Dharmakaya?"
He answered, "The flowering hedge surrounding the privy."

The question "What is Buddha?" is answered with an absurd, shocking statement: "The flowering hedge around the privy." The meaning is beyond the literal, beyond just pointing to an object as direct reference. The Dharmakaya is universal: both barking dog and growing tree are Buddha from this perspective. But it is not a literal pointing. The koan invites us to symbolize and conceive at a different level of comprehension, often with a sense of humor.

Kikan Koans

The Kikan koans aid the Zen meditator in discerning the links, the interrelationship between true nature within and everyday phenomena without. The experience of our inner true nature must be brought back into our experience of the world again. Otherwise, the world seems flat and unreal, and objects seem inconsequential and meaningless. Instead enlightenment must continue to shine, to illuminate so the world and our relationship to it can be transformed in everyday life. This koan group is one of differentiation. We must know who we are as one with Mind without also losing our understanding of how we are unique. True nature has been experienced, but now a more comprehensive and inclusive understanding is called for. How is the unique a meaningful part of a larger whole?

"Who was Bodhidharma?" asked a student.
"The tea tree in the garden," answered the master.
The student felt confused.

"Please guide me to Bodhidharma's wisdom, Master," the student asked.

The Master turned toward him, then placed his palms together with fingers extended, smiled, and bowed.

Gonsen Koans

The Gonsen koans investigate words and their relationship to events for their higher, enlightened meanings. Words and language itself, in Zen, do not symbolize or define objects. Words do not refer to objects as things, as commonly thought. By using words, a process is implied: Language refers to suchness.

One of the Gonsen koans uses the story of Buddha and Mahakasyapa: Buddha taught a lesson to a group of disciples and ended his speech by quietly holding up a flower. Among all the members of the crowd, only Mahakasyapa smiled, and this silent exchange was the first direct transmission of enlightenment from teacher to student. The mind of Zen is beyond words, as Mahakasyapa understood. Words are only used as a vehicle and cannot actually convey true insight. Mind is transmitted directly. No words can express it.

Language should not separate us from our experience. Words are simply part of our experience. Words are helpful when they join us to direct experiencing. We are not separate from our essential nature; we are one with it. These koans help to communicate this unity with true nature.

Koan dialogues invite the meditator to reconsider the context (and thus the category or class) of the object pointed to. The Zen master engages us in higher levels of understanding beyond category or context. And switching levels permits unifying in a new, synthetic, enlightened perspective, in which all makes sense. Gonsen koans teach students how to switch to other, less typical levels to gain new meaning.

The stick of Ma-tzu is an example of the Gonsen koans. Ma-tzu held up a stick and then said, "If you call this a stick, I will hit you with it. If you don't call it a stick, I will hit you with it. Quickly, now, what is it?" Ma-tzu's use of language in this koan creates the threat of punishment no matter how you answer. What should you say? You are faced with an insoluble problem, a double bind, as Gregory Bateson called it, "mutually contradictory commands being given by a person in authority with the threat of punishment if both commands [are] not carried out" (Low 1995, 13). To the unenlightened, double binds are uncomfortable. They don't give meaning; they give confusion. But from a Zen master, the relationship between language use and its context in koans is a way to communicate the subtleties that facilitate enlightenment for the student.

A relationship is necessary for the double bind to be effective. Nearly all communications occur on two levels, because of the context of meaning. The two levels of communication involve the class and the member of the class. The context is the background that gives meaning. A koan remains a double bind if we are stuck within the usual use of language and its context. But koans invite us to consider a new perspective, a new meaning for the word "stick" lest we be (symbolically) struck.

How to Work on Koans

We encourage you to pick a koan case for your own meditation. One of the best places to start is with the Mu koan earlier in this lesson. But you may want to start with one of the others here that fits you. Typically students begin with one koan and spend a great deal of time on it.

Choose one and begin your meditation. Pursue your effort wholeheartedly. If you have personal difficulty with your effort, seek out a qualified Zen master to consult. They are the best source and have rigorous training in how to guide with koans.

Truly mastering a koan at a deep level is far better than dabbling in many at shallow depth. Do not rush ahead, as there is no advantage to accumulating vast numbers of koans solved at superficial levels.

Koan as a Subject for Zazen

This exercise is drawn from Zen teacher Katsuki Sekida. Sit down in your meditation position and focus on whatever koan you are working on. Imagine repeating the koan to yourself inwardly, over and over. Let the words integrate with your breathing, in and out. Listen to yourself say the word or words, syllable by syllable, keeping all your attention on the sound and the resonance. Stay focused on the sound and nothing else. (Sekida & Katsuki 1977, 16–17)

Sometimes you may want to pick a few words to focus on, other times you may choose to attend to the whole. Don't look for an answer to the koan, just focus wholeheartedly on the koan itself. An answer may spontaneously occur to you, but don't seek one. The koan will stay with you whatever you are doing. Keep working on it with aware attention maintained on the koan.

Everything Can Be a Koan

You don't have to limit yourself to traditional koans. Dogen believed that everything in life can be a koan. By cultivating continual awareness, you make the barriers you meet in life into koans to learn from. In the sense that practice is enlightenment, everything you do becomes a Zen lesson. So when you get up in the morning, pay attention and use what happens to penetrate beyond the momentary meaning.

Follow Your Search to Its Deepest Roots

The famous phenomenologist, Edmund Husserl, used to encourage his students to perform the "phenomenological reduction." Put everything you are uncertain about in brackets and search for what you consider the absolutely certain reality. Doubt everything. Consider that you could be mistaken, filled with illusions.

We experience our taken-for-granted, everyday world and believe that what we experience is real. But Husserl believed we cannot know if our experience is true to a constant reality. We must suspend belief and seek understanding through deep thought. We do not have to assume reality is constant and unchanging. Nor should we assume it is not. Start with how things seem, how we experience, then proceed from there. This search for the experienced grounds of reality is like the search for meaning in a koan. Wonder what it means and strive to understand. Then, in the darkness, may come the flash of enlightenment.

Finding Enlightenment

The Zen masters all proclaim that there is no enlightenment
whatever which you can claim to have attained. If you say you
have attained something, this is the surest proof that you have
gone astray. Therefore, not to have is to have; silence is thunder.

(Suzuki 1969, 53)

Why is enlightenment so important? If you ask an advanced Zen practitioner what he or she found from enlightenment, you would probably get the paradoxical reply, "Nothing!"

"What? Nothing at all?"

"No, nothing, Mu."

More puzzled than ever you might ask, "Why do you want to
strive so mightily to get nothing?"

But if you ask that, you probably don't recognize how important
nothingness is for everything that exists. Sartre said that nothingness
is the origin of all things. Nothingness is the source of everything.

The Sixth Patriarch Hui-neng (638–713) urged his students to look between the lines, in a sense. He taught that the essence of enlightenment is in the spaces between letters as well as in the letters themselves. If no spaces are given between words, there could be no words, only continual letters and syllables. And if there are only spaces, no words can be perceived either. Similarly, the spaces between tones of sound make music possible. The space between sounds permits rhythmic music to be heard. Otherwise, we only hear a constant noise.

Enlightenment cannot be put into words in the sense of being contained in words. The paradoxical wisdom of Zen is communicated in silence, with silence, and is found, in speech, in the silence between words.

You can think about enlightenment more indirectly. Like looking at the spaces between the words to reveal more about what something is, you can learn about enlightenment by thinking about what it is not.

Meditation on Shifting Perspective
Sometimes the background space around something helps us to see what it really is. Look at this ambiguous figure. Notice how the background becomes the foreground and vice versus. Your perspective shifts to see the square and then the X.

Consider how enlightenment is not a thing, not words, is not known, and is nothing to attain. Look at the background. Probe deeply.

Who Is Enlightened?

Anyone who wants to find enlightenment can do so. Enlightenment is open to men and women, young and old. People from all walks of life and all kinds of backgrounds are equally capable of enlightenment. You can be enlightened too.

Dogen explained it well when he said:

Notice how your perspective has to shift to see the square and then the X.
Changing Perspectives, C. Alexander Simpkins. Wood Art Hanging, Zebrawood.

Though of humble appearance, a person who has awakened to the Bodhi-mind is already the teacher of all mankind. Even a little girl of seven can become the teacher of the four classes of Buddhists and the compassionate mother of all beings; for [in Buddhism] men and women are completely equal. This is one of the highest principles of the Way. (Yokoi 1990, 61)

Individual Commitment

Zen enlightenment requires commitment, commitment that is usually expressed through the taking of vows. The vows in most Zen temples are Buddhist. Novice practitioners go through a ceremony where they take the precepts, which means that they promise to uphold certain important values. Traditionally, all participants take refuge in the Buddha, the Dharma (Buddhist teachings), and the Sangha (Buddhist community). This means that Buddhism can be a primary resource and source of support. Participants also promise not to do evil, to perform good deeds, to refrain from harming, and to help others. These promises are not taken lightly. This decisive act sets the individual on the path to enlightenment.

Advanced practitioners take more complex vows, including ethical and moral commitments. Theoretically, you could just as well take your vows in terms of a Judeo-Christian, Hindu, or another tradition. Taking of vows is a commitment that leads to transcendence of the personal ego, an important change in values.

Contemplating Vows

Think about the many ways we take vows in life. For example, we take wedding vows, we vow to tell the truth in court, and we pledge allegiance to our country. When you do Zen, you also make certain commitments. Think about what that involves for you. Consider changes you could make to fulfill this promise.

Once you make the vow, the path to enlightenment becomes possible for you to walk. But what you find as you travel along the path depends entirely on what *you* do. The quality of your meditative awareness is at the core of enlightenment. If you just walk through the process, uncommitted, without really giving one hundred percent, there is little likelihood you'll find higher levels of enlightenment. And there is still less of a possibility of maintaining and sustaining an enlightened life.

You get out of it what you put into it, so taking the vow is an absolutely essential act that unifies your actions with enlightenment. The act may be overlooked if you just read the literature or participate in the rituals. But it should not be. Ethics and values will flow naturally from taking the vows.

Zen doesn't tell people what they should experience in their meditative awareness. The awake mind is beyond simple judgments of relative good and bad. But Zen is not amoral. Zen values are absolute, so that no question of relative good versus bad remains: no alternative exists. There is no good or bad because everything shares a common nature. So since this interrelationship exists, any action you take affects everything else. Enlightened action is aware and in tune with this Oneness. Enlightenment is expressed in action, not just words, while living compassionately.

Even though the values of Zen, in theory, are not explicitly stated in a fixed code, in practice, there are exacting customs, rules, and procedures to follow. Dogen specified these carefully. Other systems such as the Kwan Um School of Zen have a precise reference manual of procedures. Soto Master Shunryu Suzuki also placed definite restrictions and rules for conduct. All of these guidelines help to set students on a path that opens the possibility for enlightenment.

Goodness is natural to living an enlightened life. If practice is enlightenment, then enlightenment is expressed in practice. All are unified; so enlightened action should be ethical and true. But true to Zen, it is not through words.

Commitment to Compassion

Compassion is enlightened sentiment. Everyone who wants to become enlightened makes an altruistic commitment to help all beings. Zen practitioners also promise not to enter personal enlightenment until all others have done so too. So, the resolve to pursue enlightenment is primary, but all true Zen practitioners vow to reach enlightenment *and* to help others. The selfless vow is a primary part of the process. Deep commitment makes a difference. And helping others, not just yourself, is important.

Expressing Compassion in Your Life

Think of ways you could express compassion in your everyday life. For example, you could let someone go ahead of you in line at the store or help someone who is carrying a heavy load. Think of what you could do, even if it seems like only a small gesture, and then when you find yourself in that situation, do it!

Doubt and Faith

> Underlying great doubt there is great satori; where there is a thorough questioning there will be a thorough-going experience of awakening. (Hakuin in Miura & Sasaki 1965, 47)

Doubt and faith are central in Zen. With doubt we begin to search. Hakuin said that a great ball of doubt is necessary, leading inevitably to enlightenment. With little doubt there is little discovery and faith. After all, if you have no doubt, why search for something more? Why not just be satisfied with easy answers, with little efforts? Great doubt leads to deep searching, and so is a powerful aid to the process. Even analytical reasoning, conducted with great persistence while doubting all that is taken for granted as true, can be useful to the process. Nothing is sacred, because everything is sacred. Once faith emerges, doubt dissolves.

Doubting Taken-for-Granted Attitudes

Think about some of the things you take for granted in your life. Question them. For example, if you always do something one way, could there be other possible ways to do it? Many of the exercises and ideas throughout this book encourage you to consider new possibilities. Keep an open mind.

Faith can be understood in the two-level sense, of the class and the members of the class. Typically, people have specific faith in something analogous to a member of the class of "faith." For example, we may have faith in a particular belief, such as faith in Buddhism or faith in Christianity. We may have faith in a person we know: We might say, "I have faith in him," or "I have lost faith in her."

Zen looks at faith differently, more as a general experience of faith, which may be expressed as a specific experience within an actual belief. Faith involves trusting in something beyond yourself. Koans and meditation encourage us toward this general, universal feeling of faith, toward a conviction that transcends boundaries. True enlightenment provides a transcendent viewpoint in which specifics have a place within a broader perspective.

How Does Enlightenment Happen?

People study, meditate, and prepare in many ways to be enlightened, but when it happens, it is in an instant. We have many small enlightenments in life, inner learnings that are felt from within and yet share a universal character. Learning to ride a bicycle provides an analogy that may help you understand how enlightenment happens. Relate this example to your own experience:

Young children often become very excited and interested in learning how to ride a two-wheel bicycle. Kindly adults will guide the process, holding the back seat and running alongside as the child peddles. The bike wobbles as the little one struggles to find balance. After a great deal of practice, one day, *it* happens. Suddenly the child is in balance, riding, and steering all by herself without realizing it. No one can balance for the bike-rider: It is an inner experience that must be personally felt. This sudden awakening to bicycle riding is similar to the sudden enlightenment of Zen. In that moment of awakening you lose your sense of self, like the child who just rides.

Soto and Rinzai: Two Traditions, One Enlightenment

The Soto lineage views practice and enlightenment as a unity. The method for practice is sitting in meditation, or zazen. During zazen, practitioners empty their minds of the usual mind chatter to allow nature to shine though.

Like the air we live and breathe or the water that is the main constituent of our bodies, enlightenment is inseparable from each moment. It is day in, day out practice. Without enlightenment, there is no practice, without practice, no enlightenment.

There is nothing to attain or gain. So in this sense, enlightenment is nothing special, and yet it is very special. Shunryu Suzuki explains this by the example of a mother with her child. Each day is nothing out of the ordinary, and yet motherhood and the love between mother and child are incredibly special and wonderful. When you take this attitude, it is a very beautiful and mysterious world we live in, and yet it is nothing special.

Rinzai also uses meditation along with active searching, often by focusing on a koan. Students may spend days, weeks, months, or even years of pointed searching and probing, filling the mind completely with deep, penetrating questions about their true nature. Then suddenly, enlightenment happens. Enlightenment is instantaneous, a quantum change from one state to another, which was always actually present, the essence within.

Rinzai literature is filled with unusual enlightenment stories. A monk had traveled from master to master, contemplating their remarks to him while he was searching for enlightenment. Then one night he stood leaning against a fence, deep in thought. The fence broke and he fell over. Suddenly he was enlightened.

Many of Lin Chi's students found enlightenment during or following a dynamic interchange or the symbolic use of the master's teaching stick. And he strongly urged greater understanding, through further dialogues. Enlightenment comes suddenly, but usually after a great deal of preparatory time and effort devoted to it.

In contrast, traditional Soto Zen doctrine is not concerned with a "breakthrough" experience of enlightenment. Rather Soto practitioners continue steady practice, moment-to-moment. They remain alertly mindful in meditation every day, quietly sitting.

Actually, neither tradition believes enlightenment is just for now without continuing to develop later. Rinzai practitioners will continue to strive for deeper and deeper enlightenment experiences. But on the other hand, Soto practitioners do not disregard continual effort either. True to the essence of mind, the true nature of enlightenment cannot be grasped conceptually nor let go of. Enlightenment is a continuous presence, inseparable from everyday life, when correctly practiced.

As it is practiced in the West, the boundary between Soto and Rinzai traditions becomes somewhat fuzzy. Modern masters in America, such as Taizan Maezumi and Phillip Kapleau, studied under both Rinzai and Soto masters. They combined teachings from both traditions to create a unique, sensible compound that does not oppose or exclude the insights of either Soto or Rinzai. Each complements the other. Each has its value and usefulness.

How a Master Recognizes Enlightenment

The Zen master can tell when the pupil has attained enlightenment, but how? There are no fixed criteria, but there are signs which the experienced Zen teacher can perceive. Enlightenment brings relaxation and transformation that is expressed physically, in posture, gait, movements, gaze with the eyes: in fact, no one particular look or expression is exactly "it," but instead, a wealth of gestures and mannerisms communicate and display the new perspective of this change. The enlightened practitioner is spontaneous but clearly responsive. This person is relaxed, able to solve a koan with an affirming response that makes sense, and can maintain mindful awareness in action (Herrigel, 1974).

Enlightenment Is One with Everyday Life

Existence precedes essence, Sartre believed. And nothingness is the basis of being, of "as it is-ness." But faith is fundamental to the search for essence, and faith is the state of ultimate concern, of centering ourselves in our everyday experience.

We must not abstract ourselves from our everyday lives, jobs, and relationships. Instead, we use them to transform. We must participate, deeply and fully.

> For a long time now I have not been taking my place as a man along with the process of change. And if I do not take my place as a man with the process of change, how can I hope to change other men? (Chuang-tzu in Watson 1966, 166)

If we engage with awareness, we discover enlightenment in this moment, here and now. We cannot find enlightenment apart from it. So we should not use special means to bring us clarity, for such techniques will separate us from the limitations of our reality at the cost of separation from the source of wisdom, the everyday.

At fundamental levels, these understandings link the different types and forms of Zen styles together. Although the outer shell of tradition or teachings may vary, the inner core does not. The inner Way remains constant, unvarying; and though the outer Way is always changing, never static, the True Way is both, and neither. Beyond contradictions and dualities, a greater synthesis emerges.

From the highest mountain peak, the world below shows its inter-connectedness; and as the horizon recedes, the links between can be seen, always present when perceived from the enlightened perspective.

Meditate Regularly!

The sure path to Zen enlightenment is meditation. Remember that the word "Zen" means meditation. Using the meditations in this book, meditate regularly. Integrate meditation into everything you do. Begin where you are, right now, and meditate.

Oneness with Nature

An Inner Resource

Ocean's tides sweep over sand
We rest in the open palm
Of Nature's hand
  —C. Alexander Simpkins

Classical science tends to think of nature as something external to pre-
dict and control. Scientists try to understand the forces of nature and
harness them for the benefit of humanity. This use of nature can be
positive, leading to many technological advances that save lives and
make living easier.

  Zen takes a completely different view of nature as something to
connect with, to become One with. Through nature we experience
our own nature, our spiritual being. When we are truly attuned to
nature, we will know it and understand it from the inside. Today
some branches of modern science, such as ecology, have adopted
similar perspectives, working toward harmony and balance with the
environment.

Bird Perched on a Plum Branch, Artist Unknown. Nineteenth-twentieth century, Japan. Ink on silk. Donor Unknown, San Diego Museum of Art.

Nature Expresses Itself

Nature expresses the sublime. A snow-capped mountain, a fragrant cherry tree in bloom, a red-orange sunset over the ocean inspires awe and reverence. Your understanding begins with simple, direct contact: becoming aware of the grass under your feet or the stars above your head.

Trying to control nature sets us apart from it. The more we strive to control, the further away we find ourselves, alienated from our own environment. Only human beings interfere with what is naturally there: "We loiter in winter when it is already spring" (Thoreau 1965, 280). We create obstructions that alienate us from our true nature. We construct barriers on the path that hinder our journey.

Reclaim your ability to respond and react directly to what is really there by getting in touch with nature. And as you reunite with nature, you draw strength from it, rediscovering your harmony with the universe. There is no conflict and nothing to control.

Fellowship with Nature

Nature is nearby, accessible, and patiently waiting. Just walk out into the woods, climb a mountain on a majestic day, or visit the seashore, and you instinctually feel something stir within. As Ralph Waldo Emerson said, "All natural objects make a kindred impression when the mind is open to their influence" (Emerson 1965, 181).

> This intimate relationship with plants [and animals] means more than a sentimental love of Nature. What is meant is a productive relationship, which discovers the essence of things, sees as it were into their hearts. Carrying "Nothing" in the heart means possessing the highest and the ultimate—"Everything," the universe itself. (Herrigel, 1958, 68)

Our relationship with nature is a kinship. It does not need to be adversarial. With enlightenment comes an acceptance and awareness of the intimate interrelationship at the heart of all things. When you let go of your separate ego, you are no longer an isolated being living alone in your own skin. You are in an active partnership with the world. If you put your toe into a pond, you cause ripples. When you understand this relationship, you can be at peace and find tranquility wherever you are.

If you go out into a forest, you will see tall trees and short ones, wide ones and narrow ones. Even within species there are differences. Yet, trees don't aspire to be tall or short: they just grow to the height they grow. There is no external standard in nature; each flower or tree expresses its own nature, complete and perfect.

Nature is tranquil, with stillness in the midst of continual movement. The singing birds, the rustling leaves, the bubbling brook evoke quiet tranquility within. Stillness in motion and motion in stillness is nature's way and Zen's way, never choosing one over the other. When you become a part of nature's calm in the midst of activity you feel calm too. A calm mind goes with you wherever you go.

Attune yourself to nature by attuning your own awareness to what is all around you. Then you become a part of a peaceful moment in nature, busy just being trees and grass and flowers and you. You become aware of the whole, experiencing the wonders of nature through your own wonder. You are not so different: You are nature itself.

Meditation in Nature

Go out in nature. Sit quietly and close your eyes. Let your thoughts settle. Listen to the sounds, feel the breeze, notice the temperature. Place your hands down on the ground and feel the solidity of the ground you sit on. Feel the air as you breathe it into your body and then back out into the environment. Can you experience the ongoing exchange between you and the world without thinking anything about it?

Let go of any thoughts about yesterday or tomorrow. Bring yourself to this moment without any purpose or goal. For this moment, don't think about yourself and set aside your usual concerns. Be fully in the present experience of being an integral part of the outdoors. Can you be completely here in nature, now?

Nature:
A Source of Enlightenment

Unique as all the plants and animals in nature are, they also share a common nature of emptiness. The flower blooms and then fades, the tree lives out its life and then dies. All form is transitory, existing as it does in one moment and dying at another, becoming part of the cycle of existence, and giving elements to the chemistry of matter. Everything shares a common nature of being in the world for a time and then not: form leads to emptiness and emptiness returns in new forms.

If you carefully observe these qualities in nature, you will appreciate this quality of being and nonbeing, form and emptiness, central to the true nature of all things, including yourself.

For Zen practitioners, nature is the source of enlightened understanding. Nature expresses itself, unconscious of itself, empty in its deepest essence. Like a play unfolding around us, we allow it to awaken our own inner nature, playing our parts in nature's play.

Zen masters through the ages have expressed their reverence for nature in its perfect unfolding as a source for enlightenment. Dogen wrote numerous poems with nature as the inspiration:

Crimson leaves
Whitened by the season's first snow—
Is there anyone
Who would not be moved
To celebrate this in song?
(Dogen in Heine 1997, 27)

Without concern for self or worries of any kind, each creature in nature lives its life as it is destined to be. We cannot help but learn from nature's ways, flowing, empty and marvelous. The acorn becomes an oak tree; the spider spins its web. When you allow the spirit of nature to affect you, you develop and grow, as you must. Meditation teaches how to let go of the thoughts that interfere.

Sensing Nature's Wonder

Go to a magnificent place in nature. Our national parks and monuments are great resources for this. Open your senses: look at the vista, listen to the sounds, smell the aromas, feel the air. Let yourself be moved by the awe-inspiring experience.

Zen Gardening

Experience Oneness with nature by directly involving yourself with nature. Gardening and flower arranging are two traditional methods to experience nature the Zen way. (For instructions on flower arranging, see our book *Simple Zen*.)

Gardening is one of the most accessible ways. Many people have a small bit of land for planting, even if it is only on a porch or indoors in pots. If you would like to experience Zen and like gardening, try one of the methods described in this lesson. Keep in mind that this is only one Way. Other lessons present different Ways. Begin with the one that suits you best. Eventually you will probably try others as your enlightenment deepens.

Designing Your Zen Garden: Mind First

Gardening with a Zen approach begins and ends with mindful awareness. Any gardening can be Zen gardening if you do it with your attention focused fully on everything you do. The form is secondary to the deeper mind that creates it. This story illustrates that the fertile seed of any garden is meditation:

Long ago there was a monk famous for his skills at gardening. The king heard of his abilities and brought him to the castle to plant a new garden.

The monk agreed to do so if the king promised to follow his instructions. The king agreed. The monk asked that certain supplies be brought to the area. Then he told the king and his men to leave him alone. When the king and his men left, the monk sat down in the middle of the plot of land and began to meditate.

A few hours later, one of the king's men peeked in and saw the monk still meditating. Later that night, the king's men looked again, but the monk was still meditating. Food was brought to the monk the following day, but he continued to meditate. Day after day passed in this way. The king began to feel impatient. Finally, he could wait no longer. The king walked up to the meditating monk and said angrily, "I brought you here to create a beautiful garden, but all you have done for the past week is sit there!"

The monk said nothing and continued to meditate. Unaccustomed to being ignored, the king said fiercely, "I give you one more day to finish the task, and then I will kill you!"

The next day the king was amazed when he came in with his executioner. There before him was the most beautiful garden he had ever seen.

"How is it," asked the king, "that you sat for an entire week doing nothing and then created this most exquisite garden in only one day?"

The monk replied in a quiet, absolutely calm voice, "You asked me to create a beautiful garden, but to do so I must first become One with the beauty of nature. Then the rest is easy."

Planting Your Garden

Clear your mind of preconceptions about what a Zen garden should look like. Rely on your intuitive grasp of nature's design. You will gradually become attuned to your inner sense. As you begin to develop your intuition of what to include and where to put it, stay attuned as you begin to create. Let the design evolve as you go along. If you maintain your sensitive attunement to what is there, you will know what you want to do. Be flexible.

Reverence for nature is reflected in how the gardener approaches the plants and the earth with respect for all living beings. Thus weeds are not yanked out, and all forms of wildlife are encouraged to live. Natural remedies might be used to discourage destructive insects, such as washing the plant with garlic or soap, or bringing in ladybugs that will eat the insects. Poisonous insecticides are not part of Zen gardening.

Keep the garden simple. Traditionally, green plants, a small ponds or waterfall, and gravel or rocks are combined naturally. A miniature tree may be planted and groomed.

Sometimes symbolic objects are also placed in the garden to signify reverence for nature. Use objects that have meaning to you or to the themes you want represented. Although a Buddha may be significant to some people, others might prefer a religious symbol from another faith. Rocks symbolize mountains, the earth, or other things.

Make the plants look like they are growing naturally in the wild. This calls upon you to be deliberately and thoughtfully spontaneous. Moss may be used and an occasional flower might be included, but color is kept to a minimum. Be sparing with plants. Do not clutter the garden.

With emptiness in mind, consider the space between things as equally important to the plants and objects themselves. Form and emptiness need each other to create the world. Be sure to have space throughout as part of the design.

Meditate through the process of planting and arranging. Move slowly with awareness. Sense the spirit of all the different components by feeling the weight, noticing the texture, smelling the fragrances, and looking at the colors. Feel the earth as you gently place each plant into the ground. Stand back and take in the whole garden at once. Use your meditative awareness as your guide. Take time, over time, to create your space.

Care for your garden regularly by staying attuned to its needs. You may want to take a little time each day to go into your garden to meditate. Look carefully at the plants to sense their needs. Attend to it calmly and lovingly. You may be surprised by the many benefits you gain from your little piece of nature apart from the stresses and strains of everyday life.

Dry Zen Gardens

Traditional gardens in Zen monasteries are often dry gardens, composed of large rocks surrounded by gravel that has been carefully raked into patterns. The monks rake the gravel as part of their daily meditative routine.

The mood of a dry garden is quiet and sparse. Rocks are grouped together, often in threes, with one large rock combined with two progressively smaller ones. They can be tilted to create interesting patterns. The gravel is carefully raked in flowing patterns surrounding the rocks.

These gardens have symbolic significance. Rocks represent the suchness or true nature of things as they appear (form). The raked gravel represents impermanence of flowing water (formlessness). It also represents the Mind.

The colors are usually dark rocks and light colored gravel. The large expanses of light colored gravel points attention to empty space. And the large dark rocks show solid form as a stark contrast.

Thus the garden can be approached like a visual koan of the interplay between form and formlessness, to be contemplated in meditation.

Contemplating the dry garden, we are drawn out of ourselves; time can appear to stand still, and with practice we move into the void and in so doing enter a higher plane of unconsciousness. (Hendy 2001, 29)

Creating a Dry Zen Garden

Create your own dry Zen garden using whatever space you have available, even a small section of your yard. Carefully pick the rocks you will use. The older and more worn the rocks, the more valued they are by traditional standards. It is believed that rocks contain chi, the energy that flows through the universe. (See *Tao in Ten* for an in-depth description of chi.) The older the rock, the more chi it has accumulated. Look for rocks with character. Find gravel that is light and regular in its color. Zen gardens evoke experiences through minimal use of color and form. So keep the components subdued.

Meditate before you begin the arrangement. First spread the gravel over the entire surface. Next place the stones. Draw from your unconscious mind as you place the stones. Group them in a way that feels intuitively right rather than intellectually correct. After you have placed the rocks, begin raking the gravel. Keep your lines continuous and rounded. Maintain your meditative calm as you rake.

Care for the garden involves regular raking. Use this as an opportunity to meditate.

Creating a Miniature Zen Garden

Through Zen philosophy one can experience the large in
the small. And in a grain of sand, glimpse the meaning of
the world. (*Amateur Woodworker*, 1997)

Many people find great enjoyment when focusing on miniatures. Some find it soothing to build miniature cars or ships. Others might enjoy dollhouses or tiny dioramas. You may enjoy creating a miniature Zen garden using sand and pebbles on a small tray to be displayed indoors on a table or in another convenient space. Gather what you need: light colored sand, up to nine small, dark-colored rocks, a tray with sides high enough to hold the sand in place, and a miniature rake. The rake can usually be found among supplies for indoor pot planting. You can also use a small brush with widely spaced bristles or a comb for raking.

Meditate until you feel calm and tranquil. Then spread the sand out on the tray so that it covers the surface with a fairly thick layer. Let your hand feel the texture of the sand. Place the rocks in groupings. Notice the weight and texture as you handle each rock. Use your intu-

Miniature Zen Garden

ition to place the rocks. Then rake the sand in a flowing pattern around the rocks. When you are finished, continue meditating as you enjoy the beauty and tranquility of your little garden.

For a variation, add a Bonsai into your garden. They are easily available or can be created. Keep it small enough to fit in with the whole. Use your imagination.

Meditation on a Traditional Zen Garden
If you have the opportunity to visit or view pictures of a traditional Zen garden, take a few moments to meditate there. Or perhaps you have created your own smaller version. Use any of these for meditation. Before you begin, keep in mind that even though the elements have been given symbolic significance, let yourself ultimately tran-

scend concepts and just experience. Perhaps different meanings will arise within you. Allow yourself to meditate freely on the garden. Enjoy the tranquility and peace of the open space, the gentle stimuli from the simple arrangement. Relax your breathing and muscles as you stay with your moment-by-moment experience: "This practice of 'entering' the landscape calms the mind as worldly cares are set aside and the limited space of the garden can appear to expand immeasurably" (Hendy 2001, 31).

Zen Arts

Creating the Uncreated

In the silence
Between the spaces
We can hear
Sounds, thoughts, pictures,
So clear.
                —C. Alexander Simpkins

The profound inner spirit of Zen finds outer expression through art. By participating in Zen art, you can have an experience of Zen. Art becomes a part of your life, transforming the ordinary into the extraordinary. You approach life with your eyes open to the potential beauty around you, creating each moment anew. Later lessons will help you on this path.

Zen art includes painting and calligraphy, music (especially the Japanese bamboo flute), temple architecture, dramatic performances and literature, martial arts, tea ceremony, crafts, and poetry, to name a few. Each art has its own unique elements, but they all share in the Zen approach, often with common features and themes. Zen is recognized in art when the artist expresses Zen qualities such as spontaneity, naturalness, and emptiness in the work.

Zen art is a way to enter into the Zen experience. All Zen arts train the mind to help students unify with deeper nature and higher wisdom. Zen is a multidimensional experience. Art not only shows a view through a window, it's also a gateway to the Zen experience itself.

The creations that flow from applying Zen are outer reflections of the inner spirit, enriching the artist. The resulting works of art also have power to enlighten the viewer as well. In fact, Zen arts have traditionally been used for meditation, to help guide the practitioner to deeper insight.

Great Zen masters have often been artists as well, in part due to the ability they gain to perceive the world in a creative concrete way, permitting Zen to manifest tangibly through all their words, actions, and expressions, including art.

Early students of Zen in temples of Japan were often assigned a Zen art as part of their training. For example, most samurai also practiced fine arts: The Way of the sword was just another side of the Way of the brush, which led to the Way of poetry. Many samurai also played the flute after practice.

Meditation on Art

Choose a painting from this book, one that you particularly like as an object for your meditation. Sit down in front of the painting and look at it, concentrating all your attention only on the painting for several minutes. Open yourself to it, allowing your reactions, your felt sense of the moment. But don't reason analytically or think about it in any abstract way. Just experience it.

Next, close your eyes and visualize the painting. Gaze at your image in your imagination for a few minutes. Let go of all thought and simply meditate on the glow of the painting, like an afterimage.

After you learn how to do this, adapt the meditation to other situations as well. Whenever you visit an art museum or view Zen art, experience it directly, meditatively. Then you may receive direct transmission of the vision of the artist.

The Qualities of Zen Arts

In existentialism, existence precedes essence. In idealism, essence precedes existence. In Zen, existence is essence. They are one, neither comes first. There is no external, higher ideal essence, and therefore, no opposite, no duality. No lasting objects exist from which an essence can be distilled. The world is One with its essence. The Zen artist expresses this unity of existence and essence in creative works.

Oneness between artist and art involves a deepfelt identification between form and spirit. As a result, the Zen artist is capable of deep empathy. For example, when Zen artists are painting a bird, they first meditate on the bird until they become so completely conscious of it, so deeply involved with the bird, that they feel as if they become the bird. From this practice, great understanding and insight is expressed in the final painting.

Zen arts share in Taoist themes but are not limited to them. Zen artists value emptiness and spontaneity, qualities of the wordless, unknowable Tao. But Zen artists also create works that are asymmetrical, with abstraction brought about by using chance and randomness.

Zen can be used creatively, for creativity flows naturally from the point of emptiness. The Zen artist enters the state of mind of emptiness for creative inspiration so it can be given artistic form.

Music and the Sound of Zen

Sound has a long tradition of activating primal feelings and thoughts. Music communicates and expresses many aspects of the Zen experience.

The flute is the oldest known musical instrument. Neanderthal flutes made of bear bones dating back more than 42,000 years have been found in caves. The spacing between holes in the flute corresponds to a distinct musical scale.

Blowing on the flute is yet another way of expressing Zen meditation. Zen meditation with the flute became known as *Sui Zen*, which translates as blowing Zen, signifying the use of breathing as it becomes One with sound. The instrument used for blowing Zen is the bamboo flute, a *shakuhachi*. The bamboo flute was played in Japan by wandering Zen monks known as *komuso*, the priests of emptiness. "Mu" in the name "komuso" refers to emptiness, as in the Mu koan. Komuso monks walked through the countryside, meditating as they played. Their hauntingly beautiful music still echoes in Zen musical art.

Samurai also played the flute, for flute playing trains breath control. Samurai played the flute following workouts to improve their breathing, an important aspect of martial arts skill. These flute-playing sessions also helped the samurai relax after their intensive physical workouts. When the feudal era ended and the samurai were no longer needed, many became wandering flute-playing monks.

Sound also found its way into poetry. One of the best-known Zen haiku poems by Basho uses sound to express a moment of enlightened experience. The simple, natural sound of a frog entering the water expresses a profound glimpse of true nature, found in nature:

> The old pond
> A frog jumps in:
> Sound of water!
> (Holmes & Horioka 1973, 39)

Sensing Sounds Meditatively

Sound can be a way to experience more deeply. Sit quietly in meditation and relax. Listen to the sounds around you. Hear the succession of sounds, the rhythms, the pitch, and the tones all as expressions of the sound of life. Can you penetrate more deeply into sound and experience sounds without labeling what they are? Feel the resonance of sensations in your body to what you are hearing. Is there an echo from your emotions? Listen for the silence between sounds as well, the rhythm of silence with sound.

Become One with Music

Begin by meditating for several minutes. Then listen to some music that you like. You may want to find some Zen music, specifically created for meditation. There are many beautiful recordings available.

Close your eyes and let yourself become completely immersed in the piece. Allow other thoughts and concerns to melt away as you become fully focused, One with the music, and nothing else.

Creating Meditative Sound

Close your eyes and hum a single note fairly loudly. Listen to the sound, feel the vibrations in your body. Keep your attention fully focused on this experience.

For a variation, use a gong if you have access to one, or tap a surface with a padded stick. Many musical sounds are available if you search for them. Attend meditatively to the sounds and sensations and follow attentively as they fade.

Meditative Musical Expression

If you are a singer or musician, sing or play a piece with Zen awareness. Before you begin, sit quietly in meditation. Let your thoughts settle and body relax. When you feel fully present in the moment, begin to sing or play. Keep your attention focused meditatively. Don't judge your performance, just express your music. When you are finished, meditate again, briefly.

Zen Painting

Zen painting expresses themes and doctrines, offering direct experience of Zen to the viewer while permitting Zen beyond words, concepts, or letters. Thus a picture is truly worth a thousand words.

Zen paintings use minimal lines, patterns, or shapes to express the vision of the artist while giving the experience to the viewer. Suzuki refers to this minimalism as the one-corner way of painting, which states Zen aesthetics in terms of a familiar Confucian concept: a concept of what is. If you are shown one corner, can you grasp the other three? The Zen painter's composition is deceptively simple: from the simple the profound grows. On the one hand, there is no need to add details to show the other corners. On the other hand, a significant detail may be the best way to indicate other corners. Asymmetrical lines in a painting sweep us into a feeling, an experience of the world that is true to Zen.

Types of Zen Painting

Traditionally, Zen paintings often depicted nature, but not as realistic representations. Instead they captured the spirit of nature in its emptiness with vast vistas, a simple bamboo, a single flower, or a solitary bird perched on a branch. Often only a suggestion of the subject is pictured, so that the full picture takes place in the Oneness between the artist and the mind of the beholder.

Zen paintings that capture a single event or a Zen action are called *zenkizu*. These works depict pivotal enlightenment experiences, dialogues between two Zen masters, and other pictures of typical Zen events.

The ox herd pictures are another type of zenkizu that tell an allegorical story. A series of six to ten pictures, drawn inside a circle, illustrates the progressive path to awakening. In this story, a young ox herd has lost the ox he is supposed to take care of. After great effort, he finds and tames it. Both become enlightened, pictured as an empty circle. In the final picture, the boy returns to the world to help others. These paintings are often presented along with a poem to help deepen the viewer's experience.

Zen painters also created portraits of their teachers or significant figures in their Zen lineage. Bodhidharma has been a favorite subject of numerous paintings, usually portraying his fierce intensity. Sometimes they painted popular folk heroes, such as Hotei, a wandering man who played a benevolent role similar to Santa, giving toys to children from a sack on his back.

An example of a zenkizu painting, showing a typical Zen event. *Monks Crossing Bridge*, Nagasawa Rosetsu. Edo period (1615–1868), Japan. Ink and color on paper. Gift of Mrs. Leon D. Bonnet, San Diego Museum of Art.

Many Zen artists also did self-portraits. Miyamoto Musashi, though a master swordsman, was also a sensitive and prolific painter, who left likenesses of himself and Bodhidharma, as well as sensitive paintings of nature and its creatures. In his later years, well into his eighties, the great Zen Master Hakuin created his own self-portrait, a Bodhidharma painting, and other meaningful scenes as well as calligraphy concerning Zen doctrines.

Abstract Expression

Zen artists used techniques in early centuries that anticipated modern artists of the twentieth century. For example, Zen-inspired magistrate and artist Chen Jung (c. 1215) was known for living simply with uninhibited fervor. He indulged in wildly creative paintings, would get intoxicated, and then used his hat as a palette knife to apply ink, splash ink on his paintings for clouds, and spit water to create mist effects. Some used their sleeves. Jackson Pollack, famous American abstract artist, similarly splashed paint spontaneously to create effects. Improvisational modern painting draws from the same wellspring as Zen.

Zen art shows the meaning behind the vision, the concrete in the abstract. So a stone is a stone, and yet it is not only that, a stone is also the universe itself, in a very real sense, through our identification with enlightened perception. A vision such as this may be rendered in paint, by spontaneous strokes, or by carefully measured strokes, once the original technique is forgotten.

Painting Preliminaries

Zen painting is usually done in Sumi ink on rice paper. Sumi ink is a compressed cake of fine black ink. When the stick is rubbed in a little bit of water, rich, black ink is created. Sumi brushes have longer handles and longer bristles than the usual watercolor brush. Various sizes of bristles on different brushes make varied effects possible. Most art stores can guide you in the purchase of the supplies you will need. For guidance on getting started in Sumi painting, consult *Simple Zen* or one of the many books devoted to this topic.

Creating a Zen Painting: From Mind to Paper

Traditional Zen paintings were done using Sumi, and this medium lends itself extremely well to natural movements of the brush flowing directly from the mind. But you can use any form of painting to create a Zen painting. You may want to work with watercolors, acrylics, or even finger paints. Some of the old Zen masters liked finger painting. Computer users may prefer to work from a computer-painting program with a graphics tablet. The point is the intent, to extend your mind and communicate your inner spirit through your artistic expression.

Readying to Paint

When you paint in the Zen way, you will go beyond technique to no-technique to express yourself naturally, without thought. This requires some preliminary practice to begin mastering your use of the brush.

Before you create a painting, practice technique in whatever medium you have chosen until you feel at ease with a few basic brush strokes. Repeat painting lines and circles using varying pressure for different thickness and textures. Keep your attention focused on your action without straining. Be relaxed and natural.

Once you can do a few basic techniques without thinking about them, create a painting. You will enlarge your repertoire of techniques over time; so don't hold yourself back from creating a picture while you are still trying to master new techniques. Remember that Zen paintings are often done very simply, using only the minimum needed to suggest the spirit of the subject.

Meditative Painting

Get your materials out and ready. Sit down to meditate. Relax your body and breathe with awareness. Then begin to paint. Let your arm move freely. Don't be stiff or jerky in your motions. Stay away from exact representation. Zen painting is like a dance or a martial art form, flowing out of the unconscious.

Keep your mind focused and open. Let the brush move and the paint flow naturally. Don't think critically about what you are doing. Stay unified with the experience of painting in the moment. Let go, be spontaneous, and allow your inspiration to move you. With nothing in mind, paint until you are finished.

Zen and Poetry

Although haiku is most commonly associated with Zen, Zen poetry may be other forms of poetry such as renga and haiga. A poem's Zen quality derives from its themes or function. Poetry may express enlightenment or be created on the spot, at the moment of being enlightened. But Zen poetry is not for only one particular goal or purpose or it would not be Zen. Zen poetry is free of boundaries that limit it to only one form, topic, or artistic theme.

Early Development of Poetry

Renga, which means linked verse, was a popular form of poetry in early Japan. Renga was often created at poetry parties where poets would gather, linking poems together in enjoyable sharing. Early creations had a formal and elegant quality, but gradually renga became more varied. The structure of renga includes three lines of five, seven, and five syllables followed by two lines of seven and seven. The pattern repeats for up to one hundred lines.

The links between verses are not always direct; the chains of association can be the ending line, an implicit meaning, a color or tone, leading to the first line of a new group of lines. The renga may then, as a result, dissociate from the original meaning of the first group of lines, creating a new unity, instead. Today's renga is less formal but retains the sensitivity and depth.

Haiku, originally called hokku, was a simplification of renga and even a simplification of the shorter verses known as tanka, which were thirty-one syllables long. Hokku consisted of only three lines of about seventeen syllables on one subject. Much later on, Shiki (1867–1902) popularized this poetic form and gave it the name haiku that we use today.

Poetry also found its way into the world of the samurai and monks who wrote haiku, death poems, and enlightenment poems, putting their pivotal moment into words. In Japan, it became a tradition when nearing the moment of death to leave a farewell poem. The poem contained a last insight, an inspiration, or some encouragement to those left behind. The death poems of Zen monks and samurai often conveyed Zen. This farewell poem from samurai Nyudo expresses his enlightenment at the moment of death:

Holding forth this sword,
I cut vacuity in twain;
In the midst of the great fire,
A stream of refreshing breeze!
(Suzuki 1973, 84)

Many haiku poets also commemorated their last moments in a poem. Here is the final haiku written by the famous haiku poet Basho:

On a journey, ill:
My dream goes wandering
Over withered fields.
(Basho in Hoffman 1986, 143)

Basho (1644–1694)

There were many great masters of haiku, but we will mention only a few masters who influenced the art and are generally recognized today.

Basho spent his early years in training as a samurai, but his master was killed in an accident in 1666, leaving Basho at a loss as to what to do. He left his home town and began traveling, learning to write poetry. He was uncertain whether this was his true calling, but his unique talent shone brightly. Basho entered and won poetry contests and soon rose to prominence. He began publishing poems early and never stopped. He interacted with other poets, creating renga and renku (shorter versions of renga). As his fame grew, he helped to judge poetry contests, from which books were published, including some of his own poems.

Basho began teaching poetry. His students felt great devotion to him and built him a little hut to live in. The hut had a banana tree (basho) next to it, and so the hut was named the Basho Hut. He adopted the name of his hut as his personal name, and he is known by that name. But Basho could not remain still in his hut. He thought of himself as a windswept spirit and so enjoyed life as a traveler, setting out on continual journeys. He observed nature as he wandered throughout Japan and wrote about it in his poetry journals. Patrons, students, and friends took care of his needs.

During one of his journeys, Basho studied Zen under Zen Master Butcho. He wove Zen themes into the fabric of his poems. Basho's insights impart a Zen moment when read. For example, in this poem, Basho suggests impermanence and direct experience without thought:

Those who see the lightning
And think nothing:
How precious they are!
(Holmes & Horioka 1973, 70)

In his last years Basho became a very famous poet. He found inner balance between his worldly involvement and spirituality. His later haiku were more tranquil, reflecting a calmer and lighter attitude to life that he finally gained, along with a capacity to transcend discomfort, using symbols and vivid metaphors with subtle artistry. Though he now had another basho hut, he continued to travel about, writing about nature and feelings until he died.

The skylark
Sings in the field:
Free of all things.
(Holmes & Horioka 1973, 111)

Other Haiku Poets

Haiku continued to be a popular form of artistic expression. Yosa
Buson (1716–1784) was one of Japan's finest painters. He painted
rocks and landscapes as living, breathing, weightless mystery. He also
adapted his creative skills from painting to poetry, giving it breathtak-
ing beauty and sensitive visual detail. Buson is also considered among
the greatest haiku poets. His style was dynamic and visual, painting
with words. Two famous statements from him express this well: "A
poem is a painting with a voice," and "A poem is a voiceless painting"
(Fontein & Hickman 1970, 14).

Two butterflies:
They dance in the air till,
Double-white, they meet.
(Holmes & Horioka 1973, 45)

Issa (1763–1827) led a life with many personal tragedies, including a loss of fortune and the important persons he cared for, but he
rose above the adversity through creative expression in poetry. His
poems are timeless metaphors, personal and compassionate. They
continue to touch the souls of readers through the ages, extending the
range of feelings about personal and universal themes.

All creatures!
They squirm about among
The flowers in bloom.
(Holmes & Horioka 1973, 31)

By the nineteenth century, haiku had become derogated as low
class literature. Shiki Masaoka (1867–1902) wrote profound and pro-

lific haiku, inspiring his readers and once again elevating the form. Although Shiki's life was cut tragically short, he left an indelible mark on haiku forever.

Shiki devoted his short life to poetry. As a young child he composed hundreds of poems in varying forms. But he found his true talent in the short fifteen syllable hokko, which he renamed haiku. He had an affinity with nature and so this medium suited him perfectly. But Shiki was diagnosed with tuberculosis and was bedridden for the last seven years of his life. He devoted himself fully to haiku, composing more than 25,000 of them. Shiki's poems expressed a sketch of real life, revealing the deeper nature of people and culture:

> As innocently as the clouds
> He tills the field:
> Under the Southern Mountains.
> (Holmes & Horioka 1973, 30)

These four masters of poetry are to haiku like Zen patriarchs are to Zen, representing a broad range of possibility. Their steps on the path helped to make modern haiku what it is today.

Poetic Use of Language

Language can be used creatively in many ways, not just for literal reference. So poetry uses language to allude to experience, by cadence and rhythms of words, like musical tones.

In Zen's poetic use, language becomes a painting, a drawing, a story, or a song. Form and formlessness melt together, so that as we experience the poem, we may enter the timeless moment. Shiki's view of haiku as a sketch of life, like Buson's view of haiku as a painting with words, opened a new way to create and use haiku for meaning.

Instructions for Haiku

Several different criteria exist for what makes a good haiku, but generally, the instructions are simple. Form in traditional haiku is five, seven, five syllables in three lines, while modern haiku varies more, with more or less syllables as needed.

Haiku express a moment of experience. This moment might be surprising, awe inspiring, beautiful, tragic, or humorous. The descriptions should not explain, just evoke.

Haiku are Spartan in the number of words, especially adjectives and images. Yet in their simplicity, a world of experience is communicated. So keep the number of images to two or less. The lines should be simple and strong. If you use metaphors, make them vivid. Imply meanings by the words, spacing, and even what is left out.

Traditional haiku always references nature and a season. Innovative, modern haiku is more liberal and expresses a personal experience, which may or may not include nature and a season. Modern haiku sometimes refer to people, animals, events, or personal experiences.

Creating Your Own Haiku

Gather a pen and paper and sit down to meditate. Center yourself in the moment, becoming in touch with what you are feeling right now. When you are ready, write your haiku.

Go out into nature and let it inspire you directly. Experience what is there around you meditatively and then let yourself write what you are experiencing.

Creating a Renga

When you are with a group of creative people, have a poetry party! One person begins by spontaneously creating a five-lined poem with approximately five, seven, five, seven, seven syllables in each line. The next person creates a new poem, linked creatively to the first one. Each person in turn generates another poem until everyone has done so. Then read the entire poem aloud and enjoy the interconnected unity you have mutually produced.

This painting with a poem is an example of the haiga style. *Flowers*, Ting Wen-wei. 1859, China. Scroll painting. Ambassador and Mrs. E. F. Drumright, San Diego Museum of Art.

Haiga: Poetry and Paintings Combined

Several other forms of art are widely used in Zen. One type is the haiga, which is a matching of picture with a few lines of verse. In haiga, the painter collaborates with the poet. Sometimes one artist is both poet and painter. A famous example is Buson who created haiga, combining his paintings with haiku.

The poem part of the haiga is a story told with a very brief few lines. The classical form is five, seven, and five, just like haiku, but modern forms vary.

Classical haiga paintings have themes of nature rendered with landscape, animals, famous people, or often plants such as bamboo. Haiga may be created using many forms of expression, including caricatures, abstractions, and other variations. A Zen moment may be expressed in this medium quite well.

Zen in Ten

Creating Your Own Haiga

If you enjoy painting and writing, you might like to create your own haiga. Either begin with the painting and then let your poem be inspired by the painting, or start with a poem and then create a painting based in the poem. You may also choose to use someone else's poem or painting as your inspiration. Let yourself experience fully what is evoked by the one piece of art to create the other.

The two should complement each other on a deep level. Be creative and enjoy the process! This can be done with a group, just like renga, except a shorter poem results. Everyone contributes to the meaning of the haiga.

Tea Ceremony

Simple Heart,
Tranquil Moment

Mossy stone basin
Standing beside
The cherry blossoms
(Basho in Holmes & Horioka 1973, 64)

A CEO of a large American company was visiting Japan on business. The president of the Japanese company he had come to negotiate with invited him for *cha-no-yu*, a tea ceremony, with a Zen master. The American felt like he didn't really have the time because his schedule was completely full. But he recognized that his Japanese business associate might be offended if he declined to go, so he accepted.

When the American arrived at the address, the Japanese businessman and the Zen master motioned for him to follow. They entered a carefully arranged garden with fragrant aromas that gently tantalized the senses. They walked along a stone path. With each slow step, the American felt himself shedding his usual hectic pace. They came to a water basin set low. The master knelt down and carefully washed his hands and face. The CEO

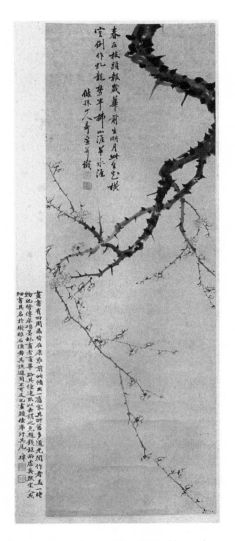

Plum Blossoms, Ting Chou. 1821–1850, China. Ink on paper.
Donor Unknown, San Diego Museum of Art.

followed, feeling refreshed and cleansed from the crystal-clear water. When they had all finished, the three men rose and continued along the path. Just ahead was a simple thatch-roofed wooden structure standing by itself with a low entry door. The American felt somehow humbled as he stooped to enter.

The room appeared stark by standards of decor the American was accustomed to, but it had an uncluttered quality that he liked. Diffused light softly illuminated a calligraphic scroll hanging by itself on a wall. A single white flower at the peak of its bloom rested in a stoneware vase on a simple wooden shelf. The master motioned for the two men to sit down on a floor mat and then placed an ordinary-looking teapot on a small fire pit. The American listened to the water bubbling.

The master sat down and began to prepare the tea, moving effortlessly yet precisely, wiping the bowl dry with a natural cloth napkin, ladling the water, spooning powdered tea, stirring it carefully with a whisk. Subdued by the sounds of clinking and tapping, the CEO felt soothed. A meditative silence pervaded the room. He found his attention turning inwards, while at the same time he felt intensely aware.

The master offered a cup of tea. The American was surprised and delighted by the delicate, subtle taste. He drank slowly, unusual for him, and found himself thoroughly enjoying every sip. The time passed quietly. The man felt completely in harmony with his surroundings. When he left he felt renewed, at peace with himself and the world in a way he had never known before.

Drinking and serving tea the Zen Way puts Zen into practice. As the man in this story discovered, tea drinking evokes unexpected depth of experience to activate deeper sources within. All that is required is that you follow along and allow the effects to happen!

Background of Tea with Zen

Tea was associated with Zen from early times in China when the monks would gather around a picture of Bodhidharma to share tea together. Over the years, monks used tea to help them keep alert during the long hours of meditation. But tea drinking did not become a Zen art until it was brought to Japan.

Mokichi Shuko (1453–1502)

Shuko was the first person to formally introduce the tea ceremony. He was a monk through childhood, but was expelled from the temple for being lazy, for he often fell asleep during meditation. Rather than give up, he went to Kyoto to continue his studies at Daitokuji, one of the Five Mountain temples of Zen. Shuko continued to have difficulty staying awake during meditation. He consulted a doctor, who prescribed tea. Shoku began drinking tea daily and nightly. He invited friends to share tea with him and served it with ceremony. People enjoyed drinking tea with Shuko, and his reputation spread. Eventually the Shogun of the area, Ashikaga Yoshimasa (1435–1490), heard about Shuko and invited him to arrange a tea ceremony for the court. The shogun liked the ceremony so much that he persuaded Shuko to do tea ceremonies full time. He gave Shuko a rustic hut where he could serve tea to all sorts of guests.

Shuko taught people to find great joy from the simple pleasure of tea drinking. He disregarded the fashions of the time to use simple, handmade, slightly imperfect utensils. His tea ceremonies gave a special experience of solumn beauty and quiet presence. Shuko's Zen teacher recognized that Shuko had found Zen enlightenment and acknowledged it officially. So Shuko is remembered as the first Zen tea master.

Sen no Rikyu (1521–1591)

Tea drinking came to full flower with the creative sensitivities of Sen no Rikyu. He developed tea drinking into the Tea Way, forever linking tea with Zen.

Rikyu became interested in tea at the age of seventeen and immediately showed talent. As time passed, the court heard of his abilities and asked him to revise the rules of tea. He took the best of the old traditions and combined them with the highest ideals of Zen. For this he is remembered as the founder of the complete art of tea.

Rikyu taught that tea, like Zen, is nothing special. A student asked Rikyu to explain the wondrous mystery of tea to him. Rikyu's answer has become immortalized in this poem:

> Tea is naught but this,
> First you make the water boil,
> Then infuse the tea.
> Then you drink it properly.
> That's all you need to know.
> (Sadler 1962, 102)

Disappointed and annoyed, the student answered, "I already know that!"

Again, Rikyu's response surprised him: "Well, if you really know it already, I would like to become your pupil! Just don't do anything bad and practice only good. Every child of three knows this but even the wisest eighty-year-old has trouble practicing it!" Exacting performance of actions may seem simple, but they actually lead to profound understandings.

Tea became fashionable for the greater society. Many noblemen and samurai became students of Rikyu. His most prominent student and greatest patron was the autocratic military leader Toyotomi Hideyoshi. Rikyu became known as a man of wisdom who was consulted for his judgments on a wide range of matters, including the arts, writing, etiquette, and eventually politics. But his political involvements got him into trouble. Eventually he came in conflict with Hideyoshi, who ordered Rikyu to commit suicide. Just before he took his own life he said, "When I have this sword there is no Buddha and no Patriarchs" (S. Suzuki 1979, 45). Thus Rikyu left the world with dignity, his last words expressing Zen.

Quiet Simplicity: Wabi

*Wabi—quiet simplicity—*is a primary quality of tea and of Zen. Often people seek escapes to help temporarily set aside problems. Natural existence becomes very complicated by the planning and carrying out of these superficial pursuits. Seeking beyond yourself leads away from what is important. The practice of Zen reveals that this quest cannot ultimately be successful. Peace of mind is not found by running away from your life.

The quiet simplicity of wabi returns you to the essentials. It gives an opportunity to be at peace. The richness of tea doesn't depend on outside stimuli but on developing inner resources. Take hold of your life from within and the outer will flow naturally.

Wabi Meditation

Wabi involves making do with less. Apply this principle to many areas of your life. Next time you are engaged in an activity, perform it with a minimum of aids. For example, if you are a woodworker, create a project using simple hand tools. For sewing, do your stitches with a needle and thread. Whatever the task, simplify it. Let yourself experience the satisfactions that come from less complicated methods and you will know wabi.

Appreciation of Simple Objects: Sabi

When you practice Zen, you learn to appreciate the simple pleasures, from the smallest to the largest. Sabi is an appreciation for a well-worn object, such as an old teapot that you have used for many years. The idea of sabi is often overlooked in modern times. For example, when taking up a hobby or interest, people think that they must purchase expensive equipment before they even get started. Novices in surfing sometimes become lost in the image of being a surfer. Such people feel they need an expensive surfboard made by a famous board maker. They want to have the right swim suit, a brand-name wetsuit, a rash guard (shirt for under the wet suit), webs to cover the hands and booties for the feet, a certain flavor and color of surf board wax, and the list goes on. The simple pleasure of riding on a favorite old surfboard wearing a well-worn pair of cut-off shorts may be lost.

Tea masters avoid the pitfalls of acquiring fancy equipment, preferring to use simple utensils. They let go of the judgments made by society about what is stylish or expensive and turn to the greater value of utensils that are unadorned, sometimes imperfect, but always useful. We can apply this to many things in life.

Sabi Meditation

Pick an object you have used for a long time. Place it in front of you and sit down. Look at the chosen object and consider its form, texture, color, or anything else you notice. Feel your sentiment for this object, recalling its many years of service to you, or any other associations. Next time you use this object, can you appreciate it because it is old, worn, and has served you well all these years?

The Perfection of Imperfection

Tea masters find sincere satisfaction in a minimum of useful, often imperfect necessities. Imperfection is valued. Asymmetry is esteemed. When something is too perfect, too round, too flat, it is often mass-produced. Tea utensils are made with the loving hand of a craftsman. So handmade pottery is irregularly shaped, with uneven glazes. This gives a certain rustic charm to them. Such imperfections point to the real world as it occurs naturally. And in this sense the tea utensils are perfect for the occasion—perfectly imperfect, as the following story illustrates:

Rikyu was invited to tea with another teaman who owned an expensive and highly prized tea caddy (a tea container). The owner proudly showed the valuable piece to Rikyu, who expressed no interest in it whatsoever. The owner felt disappointed that the great tea master seemed to disapprove, and in a fit of anger, broke the pot to bits. A friend carefully glued the valuable caddy back together, restoring it for his own use. Some time later, the friend invited Rikyu to join him for tea and used the repaired caddy. Rikyu immediately noticed it and asked, "Haven't I seen this caddy somewhere before? Now that it is repaired it has become a piece worth using!" The caddy was now handcrafted and unique. The friend was very happy to hear Rikyu's complement and promptly returned the caddy to its owner.

The significance of using imperfect utensils penetrates the meaning of Zen. The craftsmen who create such pieces are not striving for perfection, but they aren't deliberately trying to be imperfect either. The state of mind that creates such crafts doesn't make such distinctions. Perfection and imperfection—being and nonbeing, all are One. When you don't choose one or the other, you remain in the meditative moment.

Letting Go

When participants bend down to enter the low doorway of the tearoom, they symbolically leave their mental baggage outside. Once inside, everyone sits together on the floor as equals. As Lin Chi often told his students, we are all people of no rank. There is no distinction between us. Let go of your titles, your accomplishments, your failures, and just enter as a fellow human being.

The tea ceremony points to emptiness. The tearoom is sparse, with few decorations. Being in such a place with minimal stimulation to the senses brings about a tranquil feeling. To be free of objects is to be free to recognize what is beyond the material world. Less is not a loss but is truly a gain. In letting go of the known, you enter into an unknown realm of potential. Rikyu explained:

> The water that fills the kettle is drawn from the well of the mind whose bottom knows no depths, and the emptiness, which is conceptually liable to be mistaken for sheer nothingness, is in fact the reservoir of infinite possibilities. (Suzuki 1973, 298)

Participate in the tea ceremony with a sincere and simple heart. Fully immerse yourself in what you are doing, and you transcend the dualism that separates you from your actions: You and your actions become One. In this way, you lose your self-concern as you gain full presence. Paradoxically, as you fill yourself with the experience, you experience emptiness.

The Tea Way brings purity, a purification of the heart. "The spirit of Cha-no-yu is to cleanse the six senses from contamination" (Suzuki 1973, 282). Enjoying a simple cup of tea, the sense of taste is cleansed. The tea experience affects all the senses in this way. The sounds of the water boiling, the tea pouring, the aroma of the tea brewing, the warmth and the textures of the cup in the hands, in the aesthetic beauty of the simple surroundings create a meditative atmosphere. Free of disturbances, all participants open themselves to the unfathomable. For a brief period of time, this small group of people, gathered together, creates a pure moment. Tranquility arises from their innermost consciousness.

Creating Your Own Tea Ceremony

If you have one pot
And can make your tea in it
That will do quite well.
How much does he lack himself
Who must have a lot of things?
(Rikyu in Sadler 1962, 103)

You can set up a small corner of your house to perform a tea ceremony, or you can do it anywhere. If you would like to experiment with creating an environmental mood, remove decorations such as excess furniture, pictures on the wall, and unnecessary knickknacks on shelves. Light a mild stick of incense in a holder. Place a simple flower arrangement in a vase as Rikyu suggests:

Flowers of hill or dale
Put them in a simple vase
Full or brimming o'er.
But when you're arranging them
You must slip your heart in too.
(Rikyu in Sadler 1962, 103)

Hang a serene picture that has significance to you. Gather the utensils you will need: a teapot, teacups, a way to heat water, a spoon, and tea leaves in a tea container or some tea bags. Preheat the water on the stove and then place it into the teapot.

Practice making and serving tea for yourself until you feel comfortable with the process. Then invite a few guests to join you. Seat the guests facing each other. Preheat the water and bring it to the tea area, or if you have a heating device, bring in the pot of water. Set out your utensils and sit down.

If the guests are new to tea, begin by explaining briefly about the ceremony: be quietly aware and experience everything intensely. Invite the group to meditate with you for several minutes. Then prepare the tea, first spooning the tea leaves into the pot and then pouring in the water. Make your movements slow and precise without tension. Serve each guest, one by one, and then yourself last. You may like to serve a cookie to each guest as well.

Keep your mind clear, focused on your actions. Listen to the sounds, smell the aromas, savor the taste of the tea, and let yourself relax. Hopefully your guests allow themselves to experience fully as well. Everyone should refrain from talking until all the tea is served and drunk. You may want to have a brief meditation at the end.

Having been through a tea ceremony, either as host or guest, you will understand how drinking of this beverage enhances the quality of life on your Zen Path.

Martial Arts

Beyond Technique
to Mastery

Where the mind goes, the body goes; the body follows the mind.
(Miyamoto Musashi in Cleary 1993, 94)

Many years ago, a young samurai trained hard and felt very confident in his quick reflexes and powerful techniques. Periodically he would challenge well-known fighters, and since he always won, his reputation grew. He heard of a renowned Zen swordsman who lived in a remote region and decided to go there to challenge him. When the samurai finally arrived, he knocked loudly on the door. A diminutive servant answered the door and said, "Hello, may I help you?"

The samurai answered loudly, "I have come to challenge the master to a duel!"

The servant bowed calmly and said, "Just a moment, I will give him your message."

A few minutes later, the servant returned. "Sir, the master asks you to return in one hour."

土屋右衛門

Detail from *24 Warriors of Kyoto*, Tosa Mitsunori. 1583–1683,
Japan. Ink and color on silk. Gift of the Asian Art Committee,
San Diego Museum of Art.

The samurai wondered if this so-called master was just avoiding him,
but decided to give him the hour to get up his courage. The samurai walked
back to the woods and began practicing his strokes to get ready.

Meanwhile, the master instructed his servant to go out into the woods
and cut one of the beautiful orchids that grew there. When he returned
with the flower, the master placed it in a wooden stand. Then he stood in
front of it, sword in his scabbard at his belt, and meditated deeply.
Suddenly, in one graceful, sweeping motion, he drew his sword, raised it
high overhead, and came down swiftly to sever the flower in two perfect

halves without touching the stand. Then he effortlessly returned the sword to its sheath. He took the two pieces and placed them in an envelope. Then he composed the following note: "I don't think it would be appropriate for us to meet and duel."

When the samurai returned, the servant gave him the envelope. The samurai looked at the two perfectly cut flower parts. Recognizing the counter-challenge, he asked the servant to get him a flower just like the one the master had used. When the servant returned with the flower and set it in the stand, the samurai quickly drew his sword and smashed down on the flower with all his might. The flower was cut into two jagged, torn halves, along with the stand. He placed his flower side-by-side with the master's flower and compared them. Then he realized that his technique was no match for the master. He would have been destroyed. The master had spared him, compassionately.

"Tell me, servant, what did the master do to get such a perfect cut?"

The servant answered with a quiet smile, "The blade is sharp, but the mind is sharper!"

Realizing that he had much to learn, the samurai bowed and said, "Please ask the master to accept me as his student!" He became the master's best student.

This story illustrates the importance of mind in martial arts. Physical skills only go so far, and true mastery always involves the mind. Whether you are involved in the martial arts, sports, dance, or any other physical activity, you can learn more about Zen by understanding Zen in the martial arts.

Zen's Close Connection to the Martial Arts

Zen has long been intimately connected to martial arts since Bodhidharma's legendary founding of both. According to legend, when Bodhidharma made his long journey to bring meditation from India to China, he encountered many dangers along the way. He observed how the animals fought each other and mimicked these movements to defend himself. By the time he arrived in China, he had devised a system of self-defense based on the moves of animals.

Bodhidharma eventually tried to teach meditation to the monks at the Shaolin temple. But he found that the monks were passive and sluggish from long hours of sitting. They were unable to develop the alert awareness required by the dynamic Bodhidharma. So Bodhidharma taught them to move mindfully, using his self-defense movements. The monks not only became healthier from the physical exercise, but they also woke up their awareness to enlightenment. Martial arts continued its association with Buddhism in China, often practiced in monasteries.

Bodhidharma's Forms: Raise Energy and Focus Concentrations

Bodhidharma wrote down his exercises in two books. One of them, the *Book of Muscle Development, Yi Gin Ching*, survived. These exercises are drawn from this book (Yang 1990, 18–22). The exercises are not physically demanding and don't require any previous training or skill. They are an accessible way to start linking your mind with your body, similar to how more rigorous martial arts practice brings the mind and body together. These exercises also build vitality as you learn how to direct and concentrate your attention with visualization and movement.

Included are twelve exercises, called forms. Repeat each form several times, working up to as many as fifty repetitions before moving on to the next one. Do the twelve forms in sequence. Each form focuses on one section of your body and then moves the raised energy to the next part, so keep a continuous flow from form to form until finished. Stay focused on your movements. The quality of meditative awareness is most important. Over time you will bring this increase in vitality and improved concentration to your meditation.

Perform each posture by placing your body in the position described. Then imagine tightening as you exhale and imagine relaxing as you inhale. You don't really move, just vividly imagine yourself doing so as you focus your attention deeply on the area and breathe.

Form 1: Let your arms hang down, face your palms toward the floor, and bend your elbows. Imagine pushing your palms down as you exhale and relax as you inhale. Your palms and wrists will feel slightly warm after fifty repetitions.

Form 2: Without moving your arms, form fists facing down with your thumbs held out toward your body. Imagine that you tighten your fists and move your thumbs backwards as you exhale and relax while you inhale.

Form 3: Keeping your arms where they are, make a normal fist and turn both fists so that your palms face toward each other. Imagine tightening and relaxing your fists as you breathe. You will feel this in your arms.

Form 4: Extend your arms out in front of your body, palms facing each other, fists closed, and imagine tightening and relaxing your fists while breathing to move the energy into your shoulders and chest.

Form 5: Lift your arms straight up over your head, keeping your fists closed and facing each other. Imagine tightening and relaxing your fists as you do the same breathing, raising energy in your shoulders, neck, and sides.

Form 6: Lower your arms with elbows bent, arms parallel to the floor and fists near your ears, palms facing forward. Imagine tightening and loosening your fists as you breathe. This form builds energy in your sides, chest, and upper arms.

Form 7: Extend your arms straight out sideways from your shoulders with fists facing forward. Imagine tightening and relaxing your fists as you breathe to build energy in shoulders, chest, and back.

Form 8: Bring your arms out in front of your body with palms facing each other and elbows slightly bent for a rounded position. Imagine that you guide your energy through your arms to the fists while exhaling, and then imagine that you relax when inhaling.

Form 9: Bring your fists up in front of your face, fists facing out and elbows bent outward. Imagine tightening and relaxing your fists. The position is similar to form six, but the fists are closer together and

Form 1

Form 2

Form 3

Form 4

Form 5

Form 6

Form 7

Form 8

Form 9

Form 10

Form 11

Form 12

Zen in Ten

in front of your face, working a different set of muscles. Energy is raised in the arms.

Form 10: With your arms up and parallel to the floor, bend your elbows with your forearms pointing vertically. Face your fists to the front. Imagine tightening your fists and relaxing as you breathe to raise energy in your shoulders.

Form 11: Keeping your elbows bent, pivot your fists down in front of your abdomen with palms facing down. Imagine tightening your fists as you exhale and relax as you inhale. This is the first warm-down form.

Form 12: Raise your arms straight out in front of your body, palms open and facing up. Imagine lifting up when you exhale and relax as you inhale, for further warm-down.

When you are finished, let your hands hang loosely at your sides as you completely relax. Feel the flow of energy as it circulates around your body.

Martial Arts and Zen Travel to Other Countries

Zen was integrated with martial arts in Japan from its very beginnings. Many do not know that Eisai, who is remembered for bringing Zen to Japan and for founding the first lasting Zen temple, is also credited as one of the first Zen teachers of the samurai swordsmen. Eisai taught the samurai through koans and meditation.

Eisai lived during the feudal Kamakura period (1192–1336) when Japan was under attack from invading armies and internal conflicts. A soldier class of samurai swordsmen allegiant to their lord was trained to deal with the constant wars. These many samurai flooded the Zen temples to learn how to master their minds.

The samurai warriors needed to learn how to transcend fear so they could commit themselves fully in battle. Overcoming fear was no easy task, because battles were to the death. Zen offered a pathway to go beyond life and death, facing each moment anew.

Warrior koans were developed over the years to teach this large group who had very little background in Zen. The samurai were taught meditation. They were also given a koan story and then asked questions to test their understanding.

Sameness Koan

Here is an example of a classical warrior koan from this period (Leggett 1993, 56–58), created to help the samurai act bravely in battle. This koan has broad applications not only for traditional martial artists but also for everyone. In Zen, letting go of your usual way of thinking opens up a clearer intuitive sense of the world. It is not empty-headedness, nor is it thinking. Rather it is something else, another way of being aware rather than slow, plodding rational thought. Martial artists develop this kind of awareness through disciplined practice. When you learn to be One with your action, you don't have to be rocked by circumstances.

The koan is based on an incident that occurred in 1241. Zen master Rankei boarded a boat with five of his students to bring Zen to the city of Hizen (Nagasaki today). But they encountered a typhoon that sank the boat. All the passengers managed to be saved.

Koan Instructions

Read the koan and think about it carefully. Meditate and then answer the questions as warriors did centuries ago. Take your time.

The Koan

As the boat to Hizan was driven by raging winds and fierce waves, the passengers were terrified and feared that they would die. Zen master Rankei repeated over and over, "Sameness, sameness, sameness."

The other passengers were perplexed. "What do you mean?"

He answered in a calm voice, "Make your mind the same as the boat, then even if it overturns, you won't be troubled. Make your mind the same as the waves, and even the highest breaker won't frighten you. Make your mind the same as Buddha's mind, and deluded passions come to an end.

When you have the enlightenment of sameness in everyday life, then all things both great and small are Oneness."

Koan Tests

1. How do you make sameness your mind, right now?
3. In the sea of life and death, the boat (the body) meets a storm and is about to sink. Right in the moment, how do you become sameness?
4. You are meditating deeply when a blazing fire comes toward you and you can't escape. How do you come to sameness?
5. You are meditating deeply when a robber breaks in and suddenly attacks you. If you become One with him in sameness of mind, you will also be a robber. In this situation, how do you understand the true meaning of sameness?

Unarmed Martial Arts

Martial arts without the use of weapons also developed in the monasteries of China. Many different styles trace their roots back to the Shaolin temple, such as White Crane, Praying Mantis, and Black Tiger, to name just a few. Buddhist defense arts were brought to other countries as well, where they combined with the indigenous fighting styles of each country. The Okinawans developed the unarmed art of karate. Later, Gichin Funakoshi and others brought karate to Japan and developed karate-do, the Way of karate, deeply steeped in Zen and Confucian philosophy. Koreans also learned Chinese arts and integrated them into their indigenous fighting arts to create Tae Kwon Do, which integrated Zen with Confucianism.

In the 1950s and 1960s, martial arts came to the West through pioneering masters who left their countries, and from Western soldiers who learned martial arts while stationed in the Orient. For example, Chuck Norris is one familiar figure who got his black belt in Korea and returned to help popularize martial arts to the West through tournaments and acting.

Mastering the Technique of No-Technique

The martial artist learns physical techniques in the early stages of practice. This generally holds true in both unarmed and weapons arts. The grammar of movement must be carefully practiced repetitively, until it becomes possible to pay attention to more than just the details of performing the mechanics. Then the mind is free of the thought of technique. Awareness begins with general body awareness and then focuses on subtle body sensations. Eventually, shape and form of specific techniques become secondary to the light of awareness itself, which casts no shadow.

Structure of Technique

All the Zen arts, including martial arts, give a structure, a form to relate to. We know ourselves through our relationship to the world. Without some form to experience, there is no experience and no opportunity to perceive the space in between: emptiness.

Martial artists begin with structure from the ground up, beginning with how they stand while performing the art, called a stance. Placement of feet and correct balance give power and fluidity to movement.

Since martial arts began in the monasteries, defense was emphasized. Thus, blocking became a central part of training and still is. A complete set of blocks covers the whole body. Each martial art also includes a set of offensive movements, including hand attacks and kicks. Some arts also teach grappling skills such as locks, holds, and takedowns. All of these fundamentals give structure to practice for the first steps on the path.

Martial Arts Basic

If you have never done martial arts and would like to experience a martial art technique for yourself, here is a blocking technique used in many different styles. Begin standing in a horse stance, feet two shoulder widths apart, feet facing forward, balance centered. Place your left hand at your waist, fist closed. Place your right hand down in front of

Upward Block Position

your body with fist facing down. Bring your arm straight up across the center of your body away from your face as you bend at the elbow. Stop when your arm is above your head in front of your forehead, arm bent, and fist facing up. Tighten for a moment when you reach the top of the motion and then relax again. This is an upward block position.

Repeat with the other hand as you bring your right hand down at the same time. Repeat several times and you will begin to feel a rhythm.

Techniques are combined into patterns of choreographed movements called forms. These patterns carry the spirit of the art, transmitted directly, teacher to student. Practicing forms is moving meditation, Zen in motion.

Students interact in pairs in a safe, controlled situation of pre-planned exercise called three-step, to practice pre-planned attacks and defenses. The force of a punch coming toward new students often feels intimidating. They must learn to face the force, look at it directly, and block or redirect it safely. Becoming One with the situation through regular practice brings an inner transformation beyond fear. Automatic and appropriate reflex reactions follow.

Some styles include a sport aspect called free sparring, a one or two minute interval when partners exchange kicks and punches. Each tries to block the other person's attacks, but if an attack gets through, it counts as a point. The exchanges are fast and intense bringing about a true Zen moment. With no time for thought, practitioners must react directly. Training prepares the participant for what is needed in sparring, but black belts know that sparring is really a matching of minds, beyond technique: technique of no-technique.

Pathway to No-Technique

Technique points toward no-technique, by giving a focal point, a starting place. The *Heart Sutra* is a key criterion: form is emptiness and emptiness is form. When techniques are engaged in and focused on, they lead to formless awareness. In a simpler way of understanding, doing any movement exactly and precisely according to its correct form leads you beyond its form. And so, by mentally entering deeply into the movement with awareness, you emerge from inner darkness, from the sleep of unawareness to the bright light of awakening.

Entering Into Your Stance

Martial arts are always performed from a stance, but the outer form relies on the inner experience. Try these instructions for horse stance to feel this for yourself.

Stand in horse stance as in the blocking exercise. Place your balance in the center. Close your eyes and sense your balance. Shift your weight gently over your left leg and notice how your body shifts.

Stance Shift 1   **Stance Shift 2**

Weight Shifting in Stance

Then rock slightly over your right leg and feel the change in your body. Notice how different muscles tighten as you gently rock back and forth from left to right and back again. Feel your way into the center, the most balanced position where the least effort is needed, attuned to gravity. Meditate in this position until you have experienced your balanced center.

Breathing

There is no void mind without proper breathing and posture. (Kushner 2000, 43)

Breathing is an accessible connection between the outer world and the inner world. Attention to breathing is your inroad to deeper awareness and a clear mind. In martial arts, proper breathing is very important. Correct breathing keeps the practitioner calm and ready for the effort. It links mind with body and helps to direct the flow of energy. And attention to breathing concentrates the mind.

When concentrating hard during actions, you may unintentionally forget to breathe. This happens to beginners when they go through the movements and find themselves suddenly out of breath. Training with controlled breathing helps to instill correct breathing as a habit.

The inner flow of energy, known as *chi*, is directed by attention to breathing. Breathing exercises are used in many martial arts styles to raise and lower energy levels for better vitality and health. Coordinating your breathing with your movements will direct your energy and add vitality, thereby improving all your techniques.

Energizing with Breathing

Inhale as you contract or withdraw your hands and/or foot, and then exhale sharply at the point of extension. Try this deliberate breathing with the upward blocking motion you learned earlier or use movements you practice regularly. Keep your attention on your breathing as you move. Eventually both will coordinate together naturally.

Breathing with Movement

If you are a martial artist, do this exercise with a martial art form you already perform. Dancers can dance. Athletes can swing a bat, jog, or lift weights. Before you begin, meditate on your breathing. When you feel attuned to your breathing, begin moving. Continue to focus on your breathing as you perform the movements. Keep your attention on breathing as you go through the routine. Keep your breathing relaxed as appropriate to the activity, noticing it throughout. As in any meditation, if your mind wanders away, gently bring it back.

The quality of breathing is important. Breaths must not be too shallow, not too deep, not too infrequent or too frequent, exactly in accord with what is needed. If you have difficulty keeping your breathing natural, return to the meditation exercises in Lesson One of counting the breaths or simply concentrating on breathing while sitting. Then concentrate on breathing while moving. Repeat this exercise over time and feel your mind and body unifying.

Mushin: No-Mind

Martial artists develop *mushin*, the mental quality of emptiness. Mushin is the direct application of Zen to martial arts, but is not limited to martial arts. Many of the Zen arts refer to mushin to help guide practitioners in the correct approach to what they do.

Mushin is a combination of two words: *mu*, meaning emptiness, void, or no, and *shin*, meaning heart or mind. The common translation is no-mind. You might recognize mu from the first koan in the *Mumonkan* and no-mind from the *Lankavatara Sutra*.

Mushin is the state of being empty of expectation, yet fully and completely present. The martial artist trains in techniques, learns the principles of the style. But the ultimate expression of the art is to be able to let it go and keep the mind open, no-mind. Yagyu Munenori was a great Japanese swordsman who was influenced deeply by Zen. He taught many samurai how to come to no-mind in his style:

> Having seen all true principles, do not keep any of them in your chest. Let go of them cleanly, making your heart empty and open, and do what you do in an ordinary and unconcerned state of mind. You can hardly be called a maestro [master] of martial arts unless you reach this stage. (Cleary 1993, 107)

No-mind is the way to be open-minded and react to each situation with a new response, or even the same one if that is appropriate. There is no pre-patterning the state of readiness or anticipation of what to be ready for: just be ready. Mushin is focused awareness. The gap between you and others is filled only with readiness.

In mushin, your mind is not distracted by thoughts that come and go. As you perform your movements, you are not thinking about what's for supper tonight or how you felt earlier at work. You don't evaluate how you are doing, how tired you feel, or what your friends are doing. You simply perform with clarity of attention that is fully attuned to action.

Martial Arts (or Sport) Mushin Meditation

Warm up by bringing yourself into the moment for a brief time, perhaps one or two minutes, without anything in mind to do, no goal, while fully present, ready to react, but not reacting yet. When a thought arises, don't associate to it, and just let it go.

Now extend this meditation while doing a form or pattern from your martial art, dance, or sport. Can you be completely empty of any thought while being present in the movement? Don't think about your technique, just do it so completely that your body moves itself, consciously unconscious.

Mushin Speedwork

One of the benefits of mushin is a shortening of reaction times. Reactions are faster during states of open, physiological alertness.

We have all experienced this if we jump up to get the telephone when we expect an important call, but if we are busy doing something else, distracted and paying little attention, we are slow to get up and answer the telephone. So Zen meditation, focusing on the present, helps readiness, to be prepared but not distracted by thoughts and concepts.

No-mind readiness is open and effortless. Zen master Takuan, who taught samurai, called this kind of awareness the no-stopping mind. Don't attach yourself to any thought or effort. If you get caught up in thinking something specific or if you make a deliberate effort, you slow yourself down. The state of ready attention is effortless, moving freely, like a windmill turning in the wind.

No-Mind Speed Work

Even though this is a physical exercise, when done correctly it is an exercise of mental readiness. Relax for a few minutes with meditation to clear your mind. Ask your training partner to briefly hold up a target for you to hit and then move it quickly away. Hit lightly as soon as the target appears, but don't make a big effort to hit it. Just let yourself react. Keep your mind free and open. Be patient. Letting go and just reacting with full presence takes practice. Don't force it to happen. Do it in a relaxed manner.

Mushin Focus

Focus means concentrating force from an amorphous, indistinct movement to an exacting, unified point. Since form is emptiness, the more perfect the form, the more perfect the emptiness: Focus is part of perfect form. Complete, intense focus leads to deep involvement and immersion in action, whatever the action. Deep focus is meditation.

Focus is the result of intense concentration of attention on the moment of interaction, on the stance, posture, technique, everything the moment includes. Focus is highly attentive, without distractions. When focus is present, great strength and balanced power is available. Although focus practice begins deliberately, it becomes a spontaneous expression of no-mind.

A great Zen archer said, "Each arrow is final and decisive as each moment is the ultimate" (Kushner 2000, 42). Each moment in life is our first and last. Zen teaches us to bring ourselves fully into every moment, to perform each activity completely and wholeheartedly as if it were the only one. This kind of practice trains the martial artist to be ready for any situation. If you ever have to defend yourself, you cannot afford to be distracted in any way. And if you are performing for testing, you must do your best as well. Approaching each workout with full focus of mind and body will prepare you well.

Meditaton on Focus

Pick a set of movements that you wish to perfect. Clear your mind of all distracting thoughts and bring yourself fully to the present. Scan through your body with your awareness and allow yourself to relax any unnecessary tensions. When you feel calm but alert, perform your movements as if there is nothing else that matters in the world. Do them as quickly, precisely, and completely as possible. Think of nothing else. If you were distracted while performing, clear your mind and then try again.

No-Mind, No-Self: Enlightened!

Martial arts practitioners train to give themselves fully to the process of training, another application of Zen in action: Each moment is complete and new. We are all beginners each moment, all the time. And therefore, every moment is a fresh opportunity to learn. We don't need to continue to carry the burden of past failures or difficulties.

Paradoxically, letting go of your self-concern brings about better self-discipline and restraint, which are at the core of Zen.

Half-hearted effort usually leads to lackluster performance. Fully giving yourself to the workout each time leads to a loss of self-concern and great potential for change. And each technique, each form, is new learning. Giving yourself fully to practice leads to losing your feeling of limitation and trains you to let go of yourself, to forget yourself, for a time. And emptiness comes about as the cup of self-centeredness is emptied. As you make emptiness your Way you will be Zen. But when you commit yourself fully to each thing you do, you improve. Dogen's idea that practice is enlightenment applies to martial arts and to life. As you practice your martial art with absolute commitment in every movement, your practice is enlightenment.

Each aspect of living can be an artistic creation, an opportunity to lose yourself fully in the moment, to act with the sure-footed movements like a martial artist, to let the arrow shoot itself. Don't hold back your alert, awake mind.

Practice Is Enlightenment Workout

Next time you work out, approach it the Zen way. As you enter the dojo, gym, tennis court, golf course, etc., bow with respect for the place of training and clear your mind of all distractions. Focus on each thing you do. Attend to breathing. Don't make yourself try hard, just be fully committed in the moment: Perform your techniques as no-technique with mushin. You may be pleasantly surprised to discover that not only will your skills improve, but you will also get great fulfillment and satisfaction from your Zen experience!

Personal
Transformation

Flow with whatever may happen and let your mind be free:
stay centered by accepting whatever you are doing. This is
the ultimate.

(Chuang-tzu in Hyams 1982, 57)

The Gates of Heaven and the Gates of Hell

Long ago, there was an accomplished swordsman. The king heard about
his great skill and summoned him to teach his army what he knew. In those
days, you did not refuse an invitation from the king, and so the swordsman
made the trip to the palace. When he finally arrived, the king gathered all
his top guards to join in on the lesson. The swordsman said, "I can beat
anyone with only two techniques. No one can stop me."

Annoyed at the swordsman's arrogance, the king decided to test him.
He ordered his best soldier to step into the ring with the swordsman. The
king commanded, "Cut him down! You must defend our honor!"

Tiger by the Pine, Yokoku. Early nineteenth century, Japan. Ink and color on silk.
Bequest of Hortense Coulter, San Diego Museum of Art.

The soldier lifted his sword right over the swordsman's head threateningly.

The swordsman seemed unaffected and said calmly, "So be it. I can see that you have much to learn"

The swordsman knelt down, preparing to receive the unjustified deathblow and said, "Here open the gates of hell."

The king saw that he was being taught a lesson and said, "Wait, spare him." At which point the guard stepped back and replaced his sword to its sheath.

The swordsman rose, gestured widely, and said, "Here enter the gates of heaven."

The king bowed to the swordsman and said, "Please accept me as your student." He became a devoted student who ruled with constraint and compassion, seeing into the true nature of all things.

A New Perspective

Many people believe that life is hell. Buddha recognized the suffering in life but said that even though life has the potential for suffering, we can transform it. Zen practice shows how to make the transformation, opening the gates of heaven.

Zen is a unique approach to dealing with the difficulties of life. Even the darkest path brightens with the clear light of meditation. You are transformed to live passionately and competently, accepting happiness and coping with sadness in life from your calm, confident, enlightened center.

Removing Obstacles

Part of the process of transforming yourself the Zen way involves deconstructing, taking away whatever interferes with the enlightened mind. Zen master Bankei (1622–1693) explained to the many people who came to hear him speak, "Basically, there's not a thing wrong with you, it's only that you let slight, inadvertent mistakes change the Buddha-mind into thought" (Bankei in Waddell 1984, 81).

Bankei's point was that even though negative events may happen, our original mind, clear and radiant, is still there to use as a resource of stability. Sometimes we identify more with our mistakes than with our clear mind, bringing discomfort. As a result, we may think ourselves into a corner filled with problems and lose touch with the inner resource: original mind, which is always there.

Perception Is Constructed

Psychologists who study how we think are finding that perception is constructed. We undergo a continual interaction between the perceiver and the perceived, between the world we find around us and our inner thoughts about it. We form hypotheses about the world and continually test them. Based on these hypotheses, we develop certain attitudes about our world. These attitudes become fixed as concepts that we take for granted as "the way things are" (Frank, 1991). We experience our concepts as coming from outside of us. But in reality, we have constructed our concepts through this process.

Sometimes these concepts cause disturbance. Pain is a good example. Many people are afraid of pain. But they fail to recognize that there is a difference between the sensation of pain and the fear of being hurt by the sensation. In many cases, the fear of pain brings more suffering than the pain itself. People who cope well with pain know that although they feel very uncomfortable sensations, these sensations can't hurt them. They relax and let go of fearful anticipation. Then the pain, though uncomfortable, is experienced as less intense, more manageable.

Transforming Discomforts

A man sought therapy for his chronic discomfort. Sometimes he felt so nervous that he would have to leave the room, even at work. His tension was interfering with his everyday life. One night he dreamed that he was a logger whose job was to guide the logs down the river as they came along. But all the logs were converging down upon him all at once. He woke up in an anxious sweat.

He thought about how he handled things. He often avoided situations because they made him nervous. Then everything would pile up until it was overwhelming, like in his dream. Through therapy he learned to walk upstream and handle the logs one at a time, before they got bottlenecked further downstream.

Combining problems is a mental construction. Things happen, one at a time. Each moment is new. When the tense and nervous man recognized this, he was able to face his problems without adding to them, and to cope with each situation as needed, one at a time.

Meditating on Deconstructing
Using your meditation skills, sit quietly and let your thoughts slow. Focus on your breathing. Notice how each breath in and out is a new breath. Stay with this for a few minutes.

Then think about something that makes you uncomfortable. For example, think about a relationship that may not be going as you would like. Consider separate aspects of it one at a time, instead of putting them all together into one overwhelming collection. After some thought about these things, let yourself relax again, returning to your meditation. Now that you have broken down the difficulty into more manageable bits, can you begin to face each, one by one?

Make No Distinctions

> In the mysterious Oneness
> Of the universe
> None is better
> None is worse.
> —C. Alexander Simpkins

Life can be made into an ordeal by our assessments of ourselves and of others. People often judge how they are doing by comparing, either to themselves at ideal moments, or to others. They might assess that they don't measure up and then get nervous about their assessment. But make no distinctions.

Each person is unique and each situation is slightly different. Everything is interrelated, as in Indra's net—the net is lateral, not a vertical hierarchy with one above another. Farmers, for example, have their important place in the scheme of things, just as merchants do. You are important in your own way, a part of the Oneness.

Letting go of judgments and comparisons opens the possibility to see yourself more as you really are. Try to stay with concise descriptions and away from judgments whenever you are working with yourself, and you will stay closer to your true nature. Then, change becomes possible, according to your inherent potential.

Meditation without Distinctions
Meditate on what you are feeling in this moment and describe to yourself what you feel, such as, "I feel relaxed, happy, sad, a tightness in my neck, warm," etc. Notice whether your descriptions are actually comparisons or judgments, such as, "I'm not as happy today as I was yesterday" or "I feel bad." Notice the point when your meditation begins moving away from clear observations and descriptions and toward comparisons and judgments. If you notice yourself beginning to compare or judge, gently return to your description. Stay attuned to what you are experiencing.

Letting Go of Tension
Tension often becomes an unconscious habit that adds to generalized discomfort. People tense up and don't even know they are doing so. Mindful meditation helps you notice when you are tensing and gives you an opportunity to let it go.

Mindful of Tension Through the Day
As you are going about your day, take a moment to turn your attention to your tensions. Observe whether you are holding some part of your

body unnecessarily tight, for example, tensing your neck or raising your shoulders as you sit. Can you let go of this tension a bit? Breathe comfortably and let your thoughts go. Be aware of yourself without judging. Simply invite yourself to be more relaxed.

Take time out during your day to allow yourself to relax. Sometimes just a few minutes scattered throughout the day brings about a change. Eventually you will turn the tides of a tense adjustment to lower the general levels of discomfort in your life. You may be surprised that your calm center emerges of itself.

Emotions as a Doorway to Zen

Carl Jung, the famous psychologist, defined emotion as "an activity of the psyche as a whole, a total pattern of the soul" (Spiegelberg 1961, 10). Thus emotion taps into genuine being. Feelings, on the other hand, come from the ego and its interaction with the world, according to Jung. Zen meditation takes you beyond your individual ego concerns into the universal realm. Through meditation, you learn to deal with trivial feelings so that your deeper emotional nature channels into living a creative and fulfilling life.

Taming a Temper

A monk consulted Bankei for help with his short temper. The monk said, "I know I should do something about it, but I was born this way and there's nothing I can do!"

Bankei asked him, "Show me your temper now."

The monk replied, "I'm not angry now. My temper just pops out at unexpected times, when someone provokes me."

Bankei said, "Well, if you aren't angry now and your temper comes and goes, you couldn't have been born with it. The only thing you inherited from your parents was your pure, original nature. Everything else you have created yourself!"

The monk was very surprised and felt hopeful that he could change his temper.

People create their opinions, their tastes, and their insistence that things must be done a certain way. In short, they take themselves too seriously. Then, if someone disagrees with them, they feel angry, sad, or frustrated. Zen practice teaches you how to let go of the ego. Personal tastes should not be taken as deep truth. Be open to doing things in many possible ways. More importantly, do things in accord with their true Way.

Let go of your personal ego, with its strong personal preferences, and you'll find that strong emotional reactions can't be induced by others inappropriately. You are in control. You experience a reduction of uncomfortable emotional reactions.

No-Self Exercise

Think about one of your tastes or preferences. Why do you feel it is so important? What is it based on? As you explore, you will eventually come back to your ideas about yourself. I'm this kind of person or I'm that kind of person. But aren't you just a person?

Imagine that you do not have this particular preference. Won't you still be you? Recognize how you add these preferences to your fundamental nature. Can you free yourself from the pushes and pulls of preference? Meditate, allowing your mind to clear.

Next time you feel yourself becoming upset, consider whether it really matters as much as it seems to. Reconsider these issues. Change may take time.

Emptying Your Mind for Calming

Sometimes you need to let go of your feelings. Perhaps you are in a situation where being upset is inappropriate, or you may have begun to outgrow a habitual reaction but don't know how to stop doing it. This meditation helps.

When you feel upset, sit down to meditate. First, notice what you are feeling. Then, relax your body and clear your mind of thoughts. Whenever a disturbing thought or sensation appears, just let it go and return to no-thought. Keep working until the torrent slows down. Gradually feel yourself calming down.

Using Humor to Transform

Zen has never taken sides with one way over another. In fact, the comic spirit has always been part of the Zen spirit from the very beginning. Zen started with an unexpected smile when Buddha held up a flower. Only Mahakasyapa smiled back. Zen masters continued to use humor to help students break out of their patterned ways of thinking and feeling. Searching for wisdom turns you toward the profoundly spiritual. But sometimes students of Zen become so serious in their pursuit that they flatten life's multi-textures.

Jokes are often funny because they upend what you usually expect and force you to think on another level. When you get the punch line of a good joke, a sudden shift happens. For a split second you have gone beyond your usual thinking. Humor, like koans, makes you look at things differently without having to engage your intellect:

> One day, a monk proudly told Chao-chou, "I have never hit anyone with my stick!"
>
> Chao-chou's answer was, "I guess the stick you carry is just too short!"

A good laugh takes you outside of yourself for that moment. You aren't thinking, you aren't feeling, you are just laughing. In this way, laughter is not that far off from enlightenment.

Many Zen students throughout history have been transformed through laughter:

> A monk approached the great teacher Ma-tzu with a deep and serious question, "What is the meaning of Bodhidharma coming from the West?" Instead of answering, Ma-tzu knocked him over. The student jumped up laughing and said, "How marvelous!" He had found sudden enlightenment.

Later, a friend asked him about his experience. The student said, "I haven't been able to stop laughing since!"

Just as transformation may evoke reverence in the face of the sublime, it may also evoke irreverence. Don't take sides! By making no distinctions, you shouldn't choose one way over another. Life itself is your guide, sometimes funny, sometimes serious: both are possible.

When reality dissolves into nothingness, humor emerges: so, interpret either with understanding or with overstatement, and you may see the humor in the moment.

Meditation for Any Moment
Can you look at yourself with humor? We take ourselves so seriously. But if there is no ego to bruise, we live through many of life's predicaments with a smile. Try taking this perspective during any incident, any moment in your life.

Accepting Your Feelings

Japanese swordsman Yamaoka Tesshu (1836–1888) gave a Zen perspective on our human emotional nature:

> When there is happiness, be happy. When there is anger, be angry. When there is sorrow, be sad. When there is pleasure, rejoice in it. This is acting accordingly free of hindrance.
> (Stevens 1989, 144)

Problems with emotions arise when we are split off from them. Anger, sadness, and frustration are feelings that people typically do not want to experience, understandably so. But in our attempts to avoid discomfort, we may miss real fulfillment. Emotions become meaningful signposts of spiritual depth when you feel fully what you feel. Be One with your emotions and you will be in control.

Begin with an Inward Glance

Becoming aware of what you are feeling is an important component of getting in touch with your deeper emotional being. As you go through your day, take an inward glance at what you are feeling with meditation.

Next time you are feeling somewhat frustrated, annoyed, or unhappy, and before you reach the point of deciding to just indulge your reaction, stop for a moment and experiment with meditation. (As you become more skilled it will be easier to apply it when you are having much stronger intensity of emotion.)

Sit down and let yourself feel what you are feeling in the moment. Remember not to judge it, but simply sense what is there. If describing it to yourself is helpful, do so. Breathe comfortably as you sit. When you have a little more time, try the next exercise.

Oneness with Emotions Meditation

As you get used to sensing what you are feeling, try this exercise for further attunement. Next time you are in the midst of a feeling, notice if you have any accompanying sensations in your body, such as tension in your stomach, neck, or back. Become aware of what thoughts are going through your mind but try not to think further about them, just notice what they are. Let yourself feel, noticing whatever is there.

Gradually your feeling will begin to alter, usually opening a window to your deeper emotions in that moment. Stay with your feeling and perception, allowing it to change with each new moment.

Don't stubbornly hold on to your original feeling about the situation. In Zen, you don't make something rigid or fixed out of your experience. For example, perhaps you started off feeling sad because a friend left you alone, but as you pay attention, the sadness changes to a deeper sense of aloneness. Probing further, perhaps you find a more positive meaning. Strong feelings are good places to begin meditating.

Meditate whenever you are having strong feelings. Keep working on them meditatively, and eventually you will sense beyond superficial feelings to a more fundamental connection with universal nature—the Mind. Allow yourself to feel fully. Accept yourself, all of yourself, and you will come into harmony.

Seeking Help

Zen teaches humility. Even the greatest Zen masters throughout history could be humbly aware of their own limitations at times. Many of them sought a teacher or guide to help them find their way. If you have sincerely tried to work on yourself and still find that you cannot make any progress, you may want to seek out a professional.

Zen centers offer help to people who are suffering. Also, there are psychologists and counselors who are sympathetic to Zen. Some have incorporated Zen into their methods, using meditation as a key tool for healing. Mindfulness is an accepted cognitive therapy approach. Don't be reluctant to seek a helping hand when you need one. Ultimately it is your own personal journey, and set on the correct path, nothing will stop you!

Your Zen
Life

Stillness in the midst of action is the fundamental
principle of Zazen.

(Rosen Takashina, in Leggett 1988, 188)

Chao-chou asked Zen master Nan-ch'uan "What is the Way?"
Nan-ch'uan answered, "Everyday mind is the Way."

Zen puts into practice the traditional Buddhist idea that samsara
(everyday life) is nirvana (enlightenment). Enlightenment can be
found in your ordinary life as it is right now. The greatest joys and satisfactions of enlightenment do not lie anywhere beyond you.

The Zen Way is going about what you do in life but with a difference. Whatever you do is an opportunity to stay on your Zen Path:
"When you are concentrated on the quality of your being, you are prepared for the activity" (Suzuki 1979, 105). Then the quality of your
awareness is the activity itself. You do everything fully, so immersed in
the moment that you are no longer self-conscious of how you're doing.

You are just doing. This quality of activity brings a profound integration between your mind and your action, you and your life, in harmony with the world. Every aspect of your existence can be lived in this way, lighting every corner of your life.

Recreation

Begin the process of weaving Zen into your daily life by starting with something you already enjoy, such as recreation. Human beings have a spontaneous innate tendency to pay attention to things that they like. Use this natural capacity to expand Zen beyond the confines of solitary sitting in meditation into everyday life. And when you bring alert meditative awareness to time spent in recreation, you will find it more enjoyable and fulfilling.

A Vacation Moment

One person is eternally on the road but has never left home. One person has left home but is not on the road. Which one is more worthy? (Lin Chi in Watson 1993, 18)

You probably know people who are always seeking exciting diversions but never really feel happy. Ultimately, true enjoyment comes from within. Perhaps you experienced this if you have ever enjoyed an experience so much that you felt like you were away on a vacation even though you didn't go anywhere. Another time, you did take a vacation but felt so concerned about a problem that you never really felt like you got away. The quality of mind brought to the experience makes the difference. Zen is a journey that you can take anywhere, anytime. No matter where you go or what you do, you can travel the path.

In spring, the flowers;
In summer, cool breezes;
In autumn, the moon;

The snow in winter,
If the mind is not clouded by unnecessary things,
This day is a happy day in human life.
(Case 19, *Mumonkan* in Low 1995, 137)

Find pleasure in the smallest things. Let each moment bring enjoyment. For that moment, be absolutely at peace. Can you feel the quiet breeze, hear a bird singing in a nearby tree, or see a cloud drift by in the sky? Even in the midst of the most hectic stress and difficulties, these small miracles also happen.

Meditation on the Small

Take a few minutes out of your day to appreciate something small in your environment. It could be a leaf on a tree, a cloud in the sky, a wild bird, or raindrops on the window. Pay close attention to whatever you choose. Relax as you focus your attention on it. Can you open your heart to its charm, beauty, textures, colors, or whatever strikes you? Enjoy the experience just as it is. Don't think about it, just allow yourself to be absorbed, like a person who can't put down an exciting novel until the very last page.

Take a Mini-Vacation

A simple excursion can bring great enjoyment even if you don't travel anywhere special. We rarely take the time to enjoy what is right there in front of us.

Take a few hours to enjoy a local spot that you may have overlooked. Perhaps it is a destination that tourists from other places come to visit. Or maybe a local park, a little shop, a museum, or even your own back yard. Go there with no goals in mind. Allow yourself to experience it fully. Notice your surroundings. Meditate to enhance your senses, and enjoy an alert calm. Don't think about the past or the future, just be there.

Zen Eating

Eating is an activity that everyone engages in, but it often takes on many qualities that have nothing to do with eating's real purpose of taking in life-sustaining nourishment. People use eating for entertainment, diversion, gratification, or even as a stress reducer. Unfortunately deep satisfaction cannot be found by piling interpretations onto your plate. Instead, discover the more fulfilling satisfactions from being closely attuned to the actual experience of eating.

Zen helps you bring eating back to just eating. You may not only find yourself eating just the optimal amount for health, but you may also be pleasantly surprised to discover greater enjoyment in your food as you become filled with enlightenment!

Mindful Eating

Pick a piece of fresh fruit that you like to eat. Hold it in your hand and look at it. Notice the colors. Feel its weight. Is it warm or cool? Peel it slowly (if it has a skin to be removed such as an orange or tangerine). Smell the sweet aroma. Then take a bite. Notice as the juice sprays into your mouth. Bite slowly, tasting awarely. For this moment, eating this piece of fruit is the only activity in your life. There is no goal, just eating. Let yourself fully enjoy it.

Mealtime

Zen temples have a ritual for eating a meal that embodies the Zen experience. Everyone sits together, facing each other in two lines. All have their own bowl and chopsticks. One monk serves the food into each bowl until the individual indicates to stop. People learn to take only as much food as they can eat, so there is no waste.

Everyone eats together in silence. You hear the clicking of chopsticks and feel a calm atmosphere. All food is completely consumed. When everyone is finished, water is poured into each bowl. The members swish it around to clean the bowl and then drink the water, wipe the bowl and chopsticks, and put them away on a shelf. Thus eating and cleaning are all done as one process. There is no distinction between the two.

Try to discover healthier eating habits. Zen discourages people from analyzing their feelings or thoughts about food. Instead, just practice. As you engage in meditative eating, you will find change takes place of itself.

Meditative Meal

Invite your friends or family to enjoy a meditative meal with you. Prepare the food carefully, making it something that everyone will enjoy. Set the table and have everything ready when the guests arrive. Explain about meditation and ask them to eat the meal in silence. Tell them to notice the aroma, the texture, and the temperature. Taste each bite. Chew the food carefully. Don't hurry. Eat only as much as needed to satisfy hunger and no more. Keep attention focused on eating. Maintain a meditative quality of mind through out the meal. When everyone has finished, clean the dishes maintaining your quiet, meditative awareness.

Household Chores

Everything you do in life can bring satisfaction, even the most menial tasks. Zen teaches us to make no distinctions. This means not to judge one act as superior or inferior to another. For example, working on an important project and washing your dishes are both just actions.

But you probably have preferences. Perhaps you love to cook but you hate to clean. Someone else may prefer the opposite. Zen invites you to set aside these preferences and mindfully attend to the present, and nothing else. Discover your true nature in any moment: all moments are equally empty of limitations and full of potential. Stay with this meditative approach and previously dreaded tasks take on new meaning, as the following story illustrates:

A student of Zen was trying very hard to become enlightened. She asked her teacher, "What is the secret of Zen?"

He answered, "Wash your laundry."

He instructed her to wash her laundry by hand. Every day she soaked the clothes, soaped them carefully, rinsed them, and squeezed the water out of each one. Then she hung the clothes outdoors on a line to dry.

At first, washing the clothes felt like an uncomfortable, dreaded ordeal. Her hands ached, her skin dried, her shoulders and back throbbed. She felt angry to be spending her valuable time on such menial work, but she kept on washing, mindful of the experience.

Time passed. The student began to notice subtle changes. She became more efficient in her work. She didn't feel like it was so difficult. She found the positive feeling generalized to all the chores she did. Her outlook had changed radically. Her teacher smiled knowingly.

Mindful Task

Pick a routine chore, something that has a definite time limit, such as washing the car, floor, dishes, or laundry; maintaining a tool; or sweeping a sidewalk. You could begin with something you don't mind doing or plunge right into something you really dislike. Get everything you need ready and sit down to meditate for a moment or two. When you feel ready, begin the job carefully, doing your best to do it well. Maintain your meditative awareness of each moment. Follow the task through to completion and then put everything away. Perform this task in this way regularly. Over time you will begin to feel changes take place.

Extend your meditative awareness into other chores you do each day. Everything is an opportunity to meditate. Each moment of life becomes a chance to express your best nature.

The Zen Practice of Work

Zen tradition has long included work at its very core. From the early days of Zen, work was considered an essential part of practice. Pai-

Chang (720–824) is credited with setting up the routines for monastic life that are still followed today. He showed by his actions how working is intimately integrated into the Zen experience.

One day, when Pai-Chang was elderly and ill, his students thought they would ease his burden by hiding his gardening tool. But instead of being grateful, Pai-Chang told them emphatically, "A day without work is a day without food," and refused to eat. The students began to fear for his health, so they finally returned his tools and let him labor in the garden. Daily life in Zen monasteries always includes daily work.

Work is an important part of living a benevolent life. Dogen said that one of the types of wisdom that benefits others is to make offerings. Earning a living and producing goods are acts of offering. What Dogen meant by giving offerings was that when we share or give, we plant a seed of good. Work is a meaningful way to use your talents to contribute to the world and make a difference.

Each person has his or her talents: Some people are naturally strong, others intuitively grasp mechanical things, and still others can comprehend abstract ideas. Each person finds expression for these talents in work. So doing your work fully expresses your true nature benevolently, which is what Zen is all about.

Overcoming Work Barriers

Working is often experienced as difficult. Work challenges our limits, calling upon us to do something in the world. Zen Master Loori said, "The things that are most difficult for us have the most to teach us" (Whitmyer 1994, 34). Work-related challenges become opportunities to practice Zen. So work is worthy of our efforts.

Monks who live in a monastery undergo long, strenuous hours of meditation, often endured with minimal amounts of food or sleep. They sometimes feel stretched beyond their limits. Work presents similar kinds of challenges. How do you respond?

Great Zen masters in history responded by putting themselves fully into the experience. Hakuin would strap himself up at night so that he could keep meditating without falling over. Dogen gave up every comfort to pursue his meditation. Zen helps you dig down deep to discover hidden inner resources you may not have known were there.

If you find that work is difficult, how can you meet the challenge? Approach life directly. Thoughts and worries are illusions of your mind; let go of them. For example, if you tell yourself how hard you are working, you split away from your direct action. A secondary problem arises, your attitudes about hard work. Some people feel angry that they have to work hard. Others feel overwhelmed. Many other reactions are possible. But all of these attitudes are diversions from the real situation of work. If you attend to it fully and alertly, work is neither hard nor easy. When working, just work.

People sometimes feel that their freedom is being restricted because work takes a lot of their time. They would rather be free to do whatever they please.

Similarly, some might find meditation instructions restrictive. You are told how to sit and what to do. In this sense meditation directions structure your experience.

Without some direction, practice gets off track. You wander aimlessly, dabbling in this and that but never pursuing anything fully. Zen uses structure and discipline to achieve meaningful freedom. Working in the Zen way structures your actions toward enlightenment. You keep returning to the situation and face yourself there, doing what needs to be done. Whether you are an executive, a worker, or self-employed, you have your part and your chance to do something with it. Every part is a central part.

Within this structure, your experience is happening right now. It doesn't matter if you are typing, reading, making a speech, sitting in a meeting, using a hammer, running a cash register, making deliveries, etc. you are free to be immersed in the present. Nothing holds you back.

Presence in Work

Infinite is the finite of each instant. (Ross 1960, 220)

Being fully engaged in your work deepens your involvement with your life. Without full presence in what you do, life passes, and you miss your chance to live fully. Working while being aware allows you to remain fully engaged in your life.

Being fully present in your work begins with meditation. Focus on your job just as you approach a small household task—with full awareness. But performing well at your job may be more complex than performing a simple household chore. These meditations intensify how you work, help you to make mindful decisions, and enhance your productivity.

Doing What Needs To Be Done

Sit at your desk, hold your tool, or do whatever brings your full attention to this particular moment. Notice how your body makes contact with the chair you sit on or the ground you stand on. Pay attention to your surroundings, the furniture, lighting, and temperature. What sounds do you hear around you?

Now let your thoughts turn to what you need to do. What emerges as most important? Centering yourself in the present moment, you know what needs to be done. As you go through your day, pause and turn your attention to what you sense, and you will keep attuned to what to do. When your thoughts leave the present, you may get off track with irrelevant concerns that lead you in the wrong direction. Keep returning to the current moment.

Sometimes you may find your thoughts carried away by associations or distractions around you. One thought leads to another, and then you are not paying attention to the work in front of you. Just as you bring your attention back to meditation when your mind wanders, gently return your thoughts to your work. If you are easily distracted, you may need to bring your thoughts back many times. Don't be discouraged or judgmental, just return to your focus. As you practice meditation you will find that you are less easily diverted.

Mastering the Working Moment

Working can be more than simply getting the job done. It becomes your opportunity to truly master your life. A job well done fulfills, whereas a job rushed through disappoints. You become One with what you do and your work becomes a work of art. What you produce expresses quality, which goes out to enhance the greater world.

Letting Go To Work

Prepare for what you need to do and then let yourself flow with the task. You have trained for a long time: Set aside any doubts or thoughts that interfere. Do what you know how to do until you are finished. Engage fully in your work.

By staying aware as you experience, you will understand what Huang-Po, a Zen master from the T'ang period in China, told his students: "Our original Buddha-Nature is, in highest truth, devoid of any atom of objectivity. It is void, omnipresent, silent, pure; it is glorious and mysterious peaceful joy—and that is all" (Huang-Po in Blofeld 57, 1994).

The Koan of Life

> Do not ask me where I am going,
> As I travel in this limitless world,
> Where every step I take is my home.
> (Dogen in Heine 1997, 67)

Mumon said every day can be a good day, but he didn't mean good as opposed to bad. His meaning reaches to the absolute quality of being expressing itself. The koan asks, "What is the true nature of this day, this hour, this moment?"

When the Dharma is truly, fully, and existentially understood, we find there is nothing wanting in this life as we live it. Everything and anything we need is here with us and in us. (Suzuki in Shimano 1995, 7)

Our world can be a source of greater wisdom. Everything in life is a koan to be solved, an opportunity to learn about your deeper being. How you respond is your choice. Zen offers the option to respond from enlightened nature.

Lin Chi told his students, "Nothing is missing! You already have everything you need to live well." But we do not always know where to look for it. Through meditation, you learn for yourself what Lin Chi means, and where to find it.

From Personal to Universal

By fully engaging in the actions of our everyday lives we discover something more: true nature, Mind with a capital "M." This vast source of potential is within, and we evolve through using it. But we have to believe it is possible for us, with our limited capacity, to be and do more.

Zen masters encourage us to let go of such limited concepts of possibility. The Zen approach encourages us to just return to things as they are, concrete: the solid ground of true reality. We waste effort being lost in abstraction, far removed from reality itself.

We are freed by staying close to what is right at hand. Then we gain strength and capacity to handle our own life and even reach out to help other people. What is here in front of us is like a Zen garden we should care for, filled with universal values. Our smaller, personal concerns are how we extend outward to the larger world beyond.

Benevolence

Benevolence involves helping others. When you are attuned to your true nature, you feel the interconnectedness of all beings. You intuitively know that when you help others, you are also helping yourself. Dogen taught his students to practice benevolence:

> The foolish believe that their own interests will suffer if they put the benefit of others first. They are wrong, however. Benevolence is all-encompassing, equally benefiting oneself and others. (Yokoi 1990, 62)

Everything Matters

Each truly benevolent act has a positive effect on the whole world. You may not believe your actions really matter that much, but they do. Every action is a part of the whole. Like a vast ocean wave made up of moving drops of water, what you do becomes part of the currents in the world. So, keep the faith. It all matters. When you understand how this is possible, you look at your life differently. Your concrete actions do make a difference, no matter how insignificant they might seem. And how you treat the other people in your life has a rippling effect.

Courageously face each situation as it happens. Don't turn away. Awareness can free you from external constraints. Stay attuned, and you gain the ability to face whatever your life brings and find fulfillment and happiness in each moment along the Way.

A Full Life

Your Zen life is a full life, artistic and creative, passionate and emotional, calm and tranquil. You live in the everyday world with your everyday mind, meditating as you attune to the profound spiritual essence of all things. By living at One with the universe, nothing stands in your way. You are the person you want to be, adding your uniqueness to the whole.

> Seize the moment
> Before it has passed
> The first opportunity
> Is also the last

Each moment of time
In itself complete
And your life's potential
Is always unique!

—C. Alexander Simpkins

Bibliography

Amateur Woodworker, www.am-wood.com. Dec. 1997.

Batchelor, Stephen. 1990. *The Faith to Doubt: Glimpses of Buddhist Uncertainty.* Berkeley: Parallax Press.

Carradine, David. 1998. *Spirit of Shaolin: A Kung Fu Philosophy.* Boston: Tuttle Publishing.

Cleary, Thomas. 1983. *Entry Into the Inconceivable: An Introduction to Hua-yen Buddhism.* Honolulu: University of Hawaii Press.

————. Trans. 1993. *The Book of Five Rings, Miyamoto Musashi.* New York: Barnes and Noble Books.

Conze, Edward. 1961. *The Large Sutra on Perfect Wisdom.* Part I. London: Luzac & Company Limited.

Cook, Francis H. 1977. *Hua-yen Buddhism: The Jewel Net of Indra.* University Park: The Pennsylvania State University Press.

Coppens, Anton Tenkel, ed. 2001. *Teaching of the Great Mountain: Talks by Taizan Maezumi.* Boston: Tuttle Publishing.

Dumoulin, Heinrich. 1988. *Zen Buddhism: A History: India & China.* New York: MacMillan Publishing Company.

_____. 1990. *Zen Buddhism: A History: Japan*. New York: MacMillan Publishing Company.

_____. 1979. *Zen Enlightenment: Origins and Meaning*. New York: Weatherhill.

Fontein, Jan & Hickman, Money L. 1970. *Zen Painting and Calligraphy*. Boston: Museum of Fine Arts, Boston.

Frank, Jerome D. and Frank, Julia. 1991. *Persuasion and Healing*. Baltimore: Johns Hopkins University Press.

Hakeda, Yoshito S. trans. 1967. *The Awakening of Faith: Attributed to Asvaghosha*. New York: Columbia University Press.

Hanh, Thich Nhat. 1992. *The Diamond That Cuts Through Illusion*. Berkeley: Parallax Press.

Harris, Victor. Trans. 1974. *The Book of Five Rings*. Woodstock, New York: Overlook Press.

Heine, Steven. 1997. *The Zen Poetry of Dogen*. Boston: Tuttle Publishing.

Hendy, Jenny. 2001. *Zen in Your Garden: Creating Sacred Spaces*. Boston: Tuttle Publishing.

Hoffman, Yoel. 1986. *Japanese Death Poems*. Boston: Tuttle Publishing.

Holmes, Stewart W. & Horioka, Chimyo. 1973. *Zen Art for Meditation*. Rutland, Vermont: Charles E. Tuttle Company.

Hyams, Joe. 1982. *Zen in the Martial Arts*. New York: Bantam.

Hyers, Conrad M. 1974. *Zen and the Comic Spirit*. London: Rider & Company.

Kushner, Kenneth. 2000. *One Arrow, One Life: Zen, Archery, Enlightenment*. Boston: Tuttle Publishing.

Lee, Bruce. 1979. *Tao of Jeet Kune Do*. Burbank, California: Ohara Publicatons, Inc.

Leggett, Trevor. 1993. *Three Ages of Zen: Samurai, Feudal, and Modern*. Rutland, Vermont: Charles E. Tuttle Company.

————. 1988. *A Second Zen Reader*. Rutland, Vermont: Charles E. Tuttle Company.

Loori, John Daido. 1994. *Two Arrows Meeting in Mid Air: The Zen Koan*. Rutland, Vermont: Charles E. Tuttle Co., Inc.

Low, Albert. *The World: A Gateway: Commentaries on the Mumonkan*. 1995. Rutland, Vermont: Charles E. Tuttle Co., Inc.

———. 1991. *The Iron Cow of Zen*. Rutland, Vermont: Charles E. Tuttle, Co. Inc.

Luk, Charles. 1972. *The Vimalakirti Nirdesa Sutra*. Berkeley: Shamabala.

Luk, Charles. 1966. *The Surangama Sutra*. New York: The Altai Press, Inc.

Miura, Isshu & Sasaki, Ruth Fuller. 1965. *The Zen Koan*. San Diego: Harcourt Brace Jovanovich, Publishers.

Nitobe, Inazo. 1989. *Bushido: The Soul of Japan*. Rutland, Vermont: Charles E. Tuttle Company

Okakura, Kakuzo. 1989. *The Book of Tea*. Tokyo: Kodansha International.

Pilgrim, Richard B. 1993. *Buddhism and the Arts of Japan*. Chambersburg, Pennsylvania: Anima.

Price, A. F. and Wong Mou-Lam. 1990. *The Diamond Sutra and The Sutra of Hui-Neng*. Boston: Shambhala.

Ramanan, K. Venkata. 1966. *Nagarjuna's Philosophy as Presented in the Maha-Orajnaparamita-Sastra*. Rutland, Vermont: Charles E. Tuttle Company Inc.

Ross, Bruce. 2002. *How to Haiku*. Boston: Tuttle Publishing.

Ross, Nancy W. 1960. *The World of Zen*. New York: Vintage.

Sadler, A.L. 1963. *Cha-No-Yu. The Japanese Tea Ceremony*. Rutland Vermont: Charles E. Tuttle Co., Inc.

Saitom, Ryukyu. 2000. *Japanese Ink-Painting: Lessons in Suiboku Technique*. Boston: Tuttle Publishing.

Sartre, Jean Paul. 1965. *Essays in Existentialism*. Secaucus, New Jersey: The Citadel Press.

Sasaki, Sanmi. 2002. *Chado: The Way of Tea*. Boston: Tuttle Publishing.

Sekida, Katsuki. 1977. *Two Zen Classics: Mumonkan & Hekiganroku*. New York: Weatherhill.

Seung, Sahn, 1992. *Ten Gates*. Cumberland, Rhode Island: Primary Point Press.

Shibayama, Zenkei. 1993. *A Flower Does Not Talk*. Rutland, Vermont: Charles E. Tuttle Co., Inc.

Shimano, Eido Tai. 1995. *Zen Word, Zen Calligraphy*. Boston: Shambhala.

Simpkins, C. Alexander & Simpkins, Annellen. 1999. *Simple Zen: A Guide to Living Moment by Moment*. Boston: Tuttle Publishing.

————. & ————. 1999. *Simple Taoism: A Guide to Living in Balance*. Boston: Tuttle Publishing.

————. & ————. 1998. *Meditation from Thought to Action*. Boston: Tuttle Publishing.

————. & ————. 1997. *Zen Around the World: A 2500 Year Journey from the Buddha to You*. Boston: Tuttle Publishing.

————. & ————. 1996. *Principles of Meditation: Eastern Wisdom for the Western Mind*. Boston: Tuttle Publishing.

Soeng, Mu. 2000. *The Diamond Sutra: Transforming the Way We Perceive the World*. Boston: Wisdom Publications.

Soho, Takuan. 1986. *The Unfettered Mind*. Tokyo: Kodansha International.

Soothill, W.E. 1977. *The Lotus of the Wonderful Law or The Lotus Gospel*. San Francisco: Chinese Materials Center, Inc.

Spiegelberg, Frederic. 1961. *Zen, Rocks, and Waters*. New York: Pantheon Books.

Stevens, John. 1989. *The Sword of No-Sword*. Boston: Shambhala.

Suzuki, Daisetz Teitaro. 1973. *The Lankavatara Sutra: A Mahayana Text*. London: Routledge & Kegan Paul Ltd.

————. 1969. *The Zen Doctrine of No-Mind*. York Beach, Maine: Samuel Weiser.

————. 1957. *Studies in the Lankavatara Sutra*. London: Routledge & Kegan Paul Ltd.

————. 1994. *The Zen Koan as a Means of Attaining Enlightenment*. Boston: Charles E. Tuttle Co., Inc.

————. 1973. *Zen and Japanese Culture*. Princeton: Princeton University Press.

Suzuki, Shunryu. 1979. *Zen Mind, Beginners Mind*. New York: Weatherhill.

Tate Gallery. 1980. *Towards a New Art: Essays on the Background to Abstract Art, 1910–20*. London: The Tate Gallery Publications Department.

Thompson, Kay Morrissey. 2002. *The Art and Technique of Sumi-e Japanese Ink-Painting*. Rutland, Vermont: Charles E. Tuttle Company.

Thurman, Robert A. F. 1991. *The Holy Teaching of Vimalakirti: A Mahayana Scripture*. Delhi: Motilal Banarsidass Publishers.

Tsunetomo, Yamamoto. 1979. *The Book of the Samurai*. Tokyo: Kodansha International Ltd.

Watson, Burton. 1993. *The Zen Teachings of Master Lin-Chi*. Boston: Shambhala.

Woodward, F.L. trans. 1960. *Some Sayings of the Buddha According to the Pali Canon*. London: Oxford University Press.

Waddell, Norman. Trans. 1996. *Zen Words for the Heart: Hakuin's Commentary on the Heart Sutra*. Boston: Shambhala.

Yamada, Sadami. 1966. *Complete Sumi-e Techniques*. Elmsford, New York: Japan Publications Trading Comnpany.

Yampolsky, Philip B.1971. *The Zen Master Hakuin: Selected Writings*. New York: Columbia University Press.

Yang, Jwing-Ming. 1990. *Chi Kung, Health and Martial Arts*. Jamaica Plain, Massachusetts: YMAA Publication Center.

Yumoto, John M. 2002. *The Samurai Sword: A Handbook*. Boston: Tuttle Publishing.